This book is intended for educational and informational purposes only. It is not legal, tax, financial, or investment advice. Financial aid policies, tax laws, institutional formulas, and college practices may change over time and vary by school and individual circumstances.

Readers should consult qualified professionals, including financial aid officers, CPAs, attorneys, or financial advisors, regarding their specific situations before making financial or legal decisions.

The author and publisher have made every effort to ensure the accuracy of the information contained in this book at the time of publication but assume no responsibility for errors, omissions, or changes in policies or regulations after publication.

Published by Auxilium Press

Author's Note

If you are reading this late at night, after everyone else has gone to bed, you are not alone.

In many families, this isn't a formal conversation.

It's a moment.

You start looking into college costs…

Maybe just to get a sense of things.

And before long, you realize:
This is more complicated than you expected.

And somehow, without a big discussion or clear handoff…

You are responsible for figuring it out.

You may work full-time.

You may manage the household.

You may coordinate schedules, sports practices, vacations, real estate decisions, and a hundred small details that no one else sees.

And now, you're expected to make sense of a financial aid system that feels anything but straightforward.

I understand that position.

I did not originally plan to work in college planning. I once intended to become a high school teacher.

I have always cared deeply about students—their futures and the doors education can open.

I graduated from UC Santa Barbara with that path in mind. But on my grandmother's advice—a woman whose judgment I trusted completely—I chose law instead.

It was stable. Practical. Responsible.

As the daughter of Italian immigrants, practicality mattered. Sicilian was my first language. If *The Godfather* and *My Big Fat Greek Wedding* had a family reunion, you'd have a pretty good picture of my childhood—loud conversations, endless food, strong opinions, and a deep belief in opportunity.

Education was not optional.

It was the path forward.

Years later, I found my way back to students and families—this time through college funding strategies.

I work alongside my husband, Dominic. He came from the business and consulting world and now helps families through our college-planning practice. You'll occasionally hear me reference him throughout the book because many of the ideas, stories, and late-night conversations that shaped these pages happened around our own kitchen table.

When I started working in college funding, what I quickly realized was this:

The families who feel the most overwhelmed are often the ones who have done everything right.

Good careers. Responsible saving. Thoughtful parenting.

They are not struggling.

But that doesn't make this decision any easier.

And it doesn't protect them from a $90,000-per-year price tag.

The information available to them is often fragmented.

In this industry, real strategy is rarely explained publicly.

Professionals often guard what they know.

As a result, families turn to neighbors and friends.

And they hear things such as:
"We didn't get any aid."
"They made less than we do and got nothing."
"Don't bother filing — it's a waste of time."

But those comparisons are almost always incomplete.

Two families can look nearly identical from the outside — same neighborhood, similar income, comparable lifestyles — and have completely different outcomes.

Why?

Because the system is nuanced.
Deadlines matter.
Forms matter.
Asset positioning matters.
School policies matter.
Timing matters.
The difference is rarely income alone.

More often, it is strategy, structure, and timing.

I am writing this book for the parent who wants clarity — whether you plan to navigate this independently or simply want to understand the landscape before making decisions.

It is not written as a disguised sales pitch.

It is not fear-based.

And it is not a promise that everything will be easy.

It is a clear, steady guide to how the system actually works — where it is rigid, where it is flexible, and where careful decisions can prevent unnecessary overpayment.

You will see what you can do yourself.

You will also see where precision matters — and where involving a CPA or other professional may be wise.

Most importantly, you will understand that the outcomes families experience are not random.

Once you understand the structure, some of that late-night anxiety begins to quiet.

Let's start there.

PART I

The Moment

I am writing this book for the person who cares deeply about their student's future.

I know you are that person, because why else would you be reading this?

You are busy. Your time is limited.

You are likely involved in your student's school, often coordinating everything else—activities, schedules, and the day-to-day logistics that keep life moving.

And now, you're navigating college finances.

At some point, you're going to have that moment.

The one that is both exciting—and a little overwhelming.

The moment when all the years—from kindergarten on—suddenly point toward a single decision:

Where will your student go to college?

Throughout this book, I'll often refer to your student—whether that's your child, stepchild, or someone else you're helping guide through this process.

Whatever your family situation, this moment is a big one.

And it's one we'll come back to again and again.

1

The $90,000 Kitchen Table

PICTURE THIS.

Your teenager—who has quietly been doing the work for years—walks into the kitchen with unusual excitement.

"Mom. Dad. I've figured it out. I want to go to USC."

Out loud, you smile.

"That's amazing, honey. What a great choice."

Inside?

Holy crap.

How are we going to pay for that?

You've worked hard. You've built a solid life. You're not struggling.

But you're not in a position to simply write a $100,000 check every year.

We hear this all the time:
"I don't want to crush my child's dream. They've earned this.

But how do we afford it?"

If that feels familiar, you are not alone.

You haven't done anything wrong.

What we're going to talk about in this book will help steady you in that moment.

THE COST DILEMMA

I used USC as an example because it has long had a reputation for being expensive.

But here's what surprises families:
It's no longer unusual.

At many well-known private universities, the total annual cost approaches or exceeds $100,000 when tuition, housing, fees, and living expenses are included.

And that number shows no signs of slowing down.

It's disorienting to realize that one year of college can cost what a very nice home once did.

Since 1980, tuition has increased dramatically—far outpacing the growth of household income.

Some studies suggest private university tuition has risen by more than 2,000% over that period. Public universities have seen increases exceeding 1,200%.

When you see those numbers, remember:
It's not just tuition.

"Cost of Attendance" includes tuition, fees, housing, meals, transportation, books, and estimated personal expenses.

I often meet families who say, "I read that the school is $14,000 a year."

When we look at the full Cost of Attendance, it's closer to $30,000.

That moment can be a real eye-opener.

If you have younger children, you start doing the math for multiple students.

If retirement is on the horizon, the timeline suddenly feels tighter.

This isn't just a budgeting adjustment.

It's a shift in financial scale.

And it has created a new category of family:
Successful.
Hardworking.
Financially responsible.
And quietly unsure how to pay for college.

I often hear parents say, "This is nothing like when I went to school."

You're right.

It isn't.

But here's what rarely gets said in that first kitchen-table conversation:
The number you're reacting to is not always the amount you will actually pay.

That doesn't mean it will be easy.

But it does mean the conversation is more nuanced than just the sticker price.

Wanting the best for your child isn't the issue.

Not knowing how the system works is…

And this is where we begin to shift the question.

Most families assume the next step is:
"Can we afford this?"

A better question is:
"How does this system actually work?"

Because the college funding system is not built purely on income.

It's built on formulas.
On timing.
On positioning.
On school-specific policy.
On rules that most families are never taught.

High-income families often fall into one of two assumptions:
We make too much—there's no point in trying.
We'll figure it out when the time comes.

Both assumptions can quietly cost tens—sometimes hundreds—of thousands of dollars.

This book is for families who have worked hard to build what they have—and don't want unnecessary tuition expenses to undo it.

If you feel "too successful" for aid but not wealthy enough to pay $400,000 for one child's education without hesitation, you are exactly who this book is for.

2

"We've Done Everything Right"

"I feel like we're going to get screwed for doing well."

That's not the exact word the parent used.

But it was close.

And it's honest.

You built your career.

You invested wisely.

You purchased additional real estate.

And now it feels like the system is looking back at you and saying: "Great. You can pay."

Meanwhile, you hear stories about families receiving significant aid.

It doesn't feel fair.

And if we're being honest, many of the decisions you made over the years were intentional—designed to put your student in the best possible position.

You chose a strong school district.

You shaped your career around stability and opportunity.

You paid for activities that built confidence, discipline, and, yes, strong college applications.

You sat at the kitchen table long after dinner, helping with math homework and editing essays.

(And if you ever felt like you were back in school relearning fractions and subject-verb agreement, you're not alone.)

You opened the 529.
You contributed consistently.
You sacrificed.

I remember sitting with a family, and the dad looked at me and said,

"So what you're telling me is… we would have been better off if we never saved a dollar for her college?"

He wasn't being dramatic.

He was trying to make sense of a system that suddenly didn't seem to reward doing the right thing.

So when the college conversation begins, and those sacrifices feel like they're working against you, it's more than frustrating.

It feels unfair.

And underneath that frustration is something heavier:
What if I can't provide what they deserve?

If that thought has crossed your mind, let me share my perspective:
The worry—and the feeling that this is unfair—are completely valid.
You are not alone in feeling this tension.
And this is exactly why I wrote this book.

In addition to running a college-planning practice, I have a daughter in college.

I do this for a living—and my heart still skipped a beat when she finalized her school list.

The difference wasn't emotion.

It was understanding.

Because, as confusing as this system can feel, it is not personal.

It is mathematical.

And mathematics, while sometimes frustrating, is predictable.

On Paper vs. Real Life

So why does it feel unfair?

Financial aid is described as "need-based."

Even when awards are labeled "merit-based," institutional budgets and "need" often influence how those dollars are distributed.

Need is calculated using a formula:
Cost of Attendance – Student Aid Index = Demonstrated Need

We'll unpack that in detail in the next chapter.

For now, here's what matters:
The formula doesn't measure how hard you worked.
It doesn't measure sacrifice.
It doesn't measure long nights at the kitchen table.
It measures reported financial numbers for a specific year.

On paper, you may appear stronger than you feel.

And that disconnect is where much of the frustration lies.

You're Part of a Growing Group

There is a wide range of families who find themselves in this uncomfortable situation.

They earn too much to qualify for significant need-based aid at many institutions—

But not enough to comfortably write six-figure checks without consequence.

It's the middle ground—even if your life feels anything but "middle" in other respects.

You may have a beautiful home.
You may drive comfortable cars.
You may take nice vacations.

And yet, the scale of college costs introduces a completely different level of financial pressure.

For many parents in this position, the deepest concern isn't lifestyle.

It's retirement.

You're closer to retirement than to the beginning of your career.

You've spent years building savings, investments, and—in some cases—real estate designed to support you later.

Now those same assets are evaluated in a formula that doesn't always reflect how liquid—or untouchable—they may actually be.

The formula may classify an asset simply as an asset.

But you know it represents long-term security.

Factor in younger siblings.

Factor in market volatility.

Factor in business income that fluctuates.

And it's no surprise that late at night—when the house finally quiets down—the conversation in your head grows louder.

Adulting is not for the faint of heart.

Here's the real truth:
The system is structured.
It follows formulas.
And you can understand those formulas.

Before we talk about strategy, we need to understand how the system is built.

Because once you understand that structure, the emotional weight of "we did everything right" begins to shift.

Let's look at that next.

PART II

The System

Have you ever been to a play or a musical?

You see the actors. You hear the music. You experience the performance.

But what you don't see is everything that made that moment possible.

The script.
The staging.
The lighting.
The choreography.

The people behind the scenes make hundreds of small decisions you never notice—but that shape everything you experience.

The financial aid system works the same way.

What families see is the award letter.

But that letter is the final performance—not the process.

Behind it are formulas, policies, timelines, and school-specific decisions that quietly determine what you're offered—and what you're not.

In this section, we're going to pull back the curtain.

I'll show you how the system actually works—where it's rigid, where it's flexible, and where your decisions can make a meaningful difference.

Because once you understand what's happening behind the scenes…
The numbers start to make much more sense.

3

Pulling Back the Curtain

Up to this point, most families approach college planning based on their own experiences, online information, or advice from friends.

That's completely understandable.

It's also where a lot of confusion begins.

Because the system has changed, and most of what is shared is either incomplete or outdated.

One of the biggest misunderstandings?

How financial aid actually works.

So let's pull back the curtain and walk through it together.

Two Applications. Two Systems.

Most families assume there is one financial aid system.

There isn't.

The first—and most widely known—is the FAFSA (Free Application for Federal Student Aid).

This is the federal formula used to determine eligibility for financial aid.

In simple terms, it's the government's way of estimating what a family can contribute toward college.

And it works the same whether you live in Omaha, Nebraska, or Beverly Hills, California.

Then there's the second system—the CSS Profile.

I often call it FAFSA's more invasive cousin.

The CSS Profile is administered by the College Board (the same organization behind the SAT and AP exams) and is used by roughly 300 schools—primarily private universities, with a few public schools mixed in.

Here's the key difference:
The FAFSA is a standardized federal formula.
The CSS Profile is an institutional one.

And that difference matters.

Because schools using the CSS Profile can ask for more information —and interpret it differently.

For example:

- FAFSA **does not** include your primary residence or retirement accounts
- CSS Profile often **does**

Schools can also customize their version of the CSS.

Some of those questions can get… detailed.

For example, Harvard asks for the make and model of your vehicles.

That might feel odd if you're driving a two-year-old Tesla.

But if you own a collection of high-value cars, the question makes more sense.

Here's how this typically plays out:

- Some schools use **FAFSA only**
- Some rely heavily on the **CSS Profile**
- Some use **both**

If a school requires the CSS Profile, you will almost always be completing both applications.

Another important note:
Many CSS schools require financial information from **both biological parents,** regardless of marital status or relationship.

All of this affects your outcome.

This is why comparing your situation to someone else's experience rarely works.

Two families can appear nearly identical, yet experience completely different outcomes, depending on the system used.

The Number That Drives Everything

There's one number that sits at the center of almost every financial aid decision:

The **Student Aid Index,** or SAI.

If you've been through this before, you might remember it as the **Expected Family Contribution (EFC).**

Same concept. Different name.

This is the number the system uses to estimate your family's contribution.

Put another way, it's the number the government *thinks* your family can afford to pay for college.

And it plugs directly into the core formula:

Cost of Attendance – SAI = Demonstrated Need

Simple on paper.

More complicated in reality.

The First Surprise

Let's walk through a simple example.

A public university has a Cost of Attendance of **$30,000.**

Your family's SAI is **$20,000.**

That leaves **$10,000 in demonstrated need.**

Now here's the part many families don't realize:
Schools don't have to meet all of that need.

Let's say this school meets **50%.**

That means you receive **$5,000 in aid.**

But even that isn't what it seems.

Because not all "aid" is free money or gift aid.

At many public schools:

- About half may be **grants**
- The other half may be **loans**

So your actual breakdown might look like:

- $2,500 grant (free money)
- $2,500 loan (you repay later)

Which means your real out-of-pocket cost becomes:

$30,000 – $2,500 = $27,500 per year

Now let's compare that to a private school.

Same SAI: **$20,000**

But the Cost of Attendance is **$70,000**

That creates **$50,000 in need.**

Many private schools meet **90% or more** of need.

Let's say this one meets **92%**

That's **$46,000 in aid.**

And in many cases, most of that is **grant money.**

So now your cost becomes:
$70,000 – $46,000 = $24,000

The "more expensive" school…

Is actually cheaper.

And we see it all the time.

Sticker price and actual cost are not the same thing.

The Role Schools Play

Here's something important to understand:

The government calculates need.
But schools decide how to allocate it.

That's why outcomes vary so much.

On average:

- Public schools meet about **50% of the need**
- Private schools often meet **90% or more**

And even within that:

- Public schools often offer **more loans**
- Private schools often offer **more grant aid**

There are other factors at play, too:

- **Need-blind vs. need-aware admissions**
- **Endowment size**
- **Institutional priorities**
- **State funding for public schools**

All of these influence what you're offered.

Which is why this process isn't just about income.

It's about how the system is structured—and how each school applies it.

The government calculates need.
Schools decide what to do with it.

Positioning & Choices

Now you can start to see why everything we've talked about matters.

Income matters.
Assets matter.
Timing matters—often more than families expect.
And school selection plays a major role.

Because each of those factors influences one of two things:

- Your **SAI**
- Or how a school responds to it

School selection affects both:

- The Cost of Attendance
- The extent to which your need is met

Two families who appear identical on the surface…
Can end up in completely different positions.

It's like trying to recreate someone's house from a photo of the front.

You can see the outside.

But you have no idea what's behind the walls.

The good news?

There is a structure to all of this.

And once you understand it, you can start making decisions with far more clarity.

In the next chapter, we'll start breaking that down into something you can actually use.

4

The Four Factors That Shape the Outcome

In the previous chapter, you saw that:

- FAFSA and CSS are very different systems.
- Schools decide how much aid they will provide.
- The sticker price is not always what a family actually pays.

Contrary to what many people believe, the amount a family ultimately pays for college is rarely driven by a single factor, such as income or assets.

It's the result of several factors working together.

And once you start to understand these factors, the system makes much more sense.

A Different Way to Look at It

One way to think about this is to picture your car's dashboard.

When you're driving, you don't see the engine. There are dozens of systems working together under the hood.

What you do see are the gauges:

Your speed.
Your fuel level.
Your direction.
And whether something needs attention.

The financial aid system works in a similar way.

Much is happening behind the scenes that you'll never fully see.

For many families, the process feels like this:

You fill out the FAFSA.
You apply to a few schools.
And then you wait.

Sometimes for months.

If you don't understand how the system works, it can feel like you've entered your information into a machine…
…and you're just waiting to see what comes out.

Why It Still Seems Confusing

Some families try to go deeper.

They research financial aid.
They read articles.
They listen to podcasts.

They start to understand aspects of the "engine."

But even then, the strategy can still feel unclear.

While the formulas can be complex,
just a handful of key factors drive most outcomes.

These are the gauges on the dashboard.

The Four That Matter Most

For most families, four factors carry the most weight:

Income

How much the system believes your family earns.

- What actually counts as income?
- Can this be influenced as a W-2 employee?
- What if you earn well but live in a high-cost area?

Assets

What the formulas consider available resources.

- How are savings accounts treated?
- What about rental properties?
- Does a 529 plan help?
- What happens to retirement accounts?

Timing

When financial events show up in the formulas.

- Which years do schools look at?
- What happens if you have an unusual year?
- Is this evaluated once or every year?

School Selection

Where your student applies—and how those schools award aid.

- Are public schools always cheaper?
- What happens with out-of-state options?

- How do you identify more generous schools?

When families don't understand how these pieces fit together, we hear things like:

"The system feels random."
"Other families just got lucky."
"It's impossible to predict."

The Shift

Once you start to understand these levers…
Something shifts.

You begin to see why two families who appear nearly identical on the surface can end up with very different outcomes.

And more importantly—

It starts to feel less random.

Less like luck.

And, for many families…

A little less unfair.

Their shoulders relax.

The stress eases just a bit.

And the feeling of having no control begins to turn into something else:

Clarity.

And with that clarity comes something even more valuable:

a sense that you're no longer just reacting—you're making decisions with intention.

My goal is to help you build on that clarity as we move forward.

In the next few chapters, we're going to break down each of these four factors—one at a time—so you can see how they influence your outcome and where you can make thoughtful, strategic decisions.

We'll start with the one most families focus on first:

Income.

5

Income

It may seem that this is one of the simplest parts of the system. Income.

It's a word we all know. You probably understood it long before you earned your first paycheck.

But in the financial aid world, that familiar concept gets redefined.

Ask someone what their income is, and they'll usually tell you:

- Their salary
- Salary plus bonus
- What's on their W-2
- Or, if self-employed, what the business makes

But the financial aid system doesn't really use those definitions.

The number that matters most is your **Adjusted Gross Income—commonly called AGI.**

Historically, this appeared on Line 11 of the IRS Form 1040.

With newer tax forms, some families may now see separate lines for AGI and Modified Adjusted Gross Income (MAGI), particularly after recent tax law changes affecting overtime, tips, and other deductions.

For FAFSA purposes, the AGI figure is generally the key number.

CSS schools may also look beyond AGI if they believe other adjustments or deductions (MAGI) affect available cash flow differently from the FAFSA formula.

Once you understand how that number is calculated—and why schools care about it—a lot of the system starts to make more sense.

When Income Is Considered

Another surprise for many families is which year's income schools actually use.

It's not the year your student starts college.

Instead, the system uses what's called the **"prior-prior year."**

In simple terms, that means your tax return from two years earlier.

For example:

- Start college in **2029** → FAFSA uses **2027** income
- Start college in **2030** → FAFSA uses **2028** income

Another way to think about it:

The income used for the first year typically covers the period from the **second half of the student's sophomore year through the first half of their junior year of high school.**

So if your student is in that window now…

You still have time.

But not much.

One more important point:

Financial aid isn't a one-time calculation.
It's recalculated every year using a new tax return.

Which means your decisions don't just impact year one—they can affect all four years.

Above-the-Line vs. Below-the-Line

To simplify how taxes work, think in terms of two types of deductions:

- **Above-the-line**
- **Below-the-line**

The "line" is your AGI—Line 11a on your tax return.

Most deductions people are familiar with—like mortgage interest or certain credits—occur *after* AGI is calculated.

These are below-the-line.

They can lower your tax bill,
but they do **not** change the number used by the financial aid system.

Above-the-line deductions are different.

They reduce your income *before* AGI is calculated.

They can directly impact the income figure considered by financial aid.

For W-2 employees, there are typically limited options.

One common example is a retirement contribution, such as a 401(k).

For business owners, the situation can look very different.

Income flows from the business to the personal return and may include:

- Business losses
- Health insurance premiums
- Self-employed retirement contributions

These can significantly affect AGI.

A quick note:

I'm not a CPA or tax professional. This is educational guidance based on experience. Always consult a qualified professional before making tax decisions.

"What If I Don't Own a Business?"

You might be thinking:
"Great... but I don't own a business."

That doesn't automatically mean you're out of options.

In fact, many families already have something that could become a business.

We've worked with:

- A father who loved woodworking and began selling custom furniture
- A parent who transitioned into consulting after leaving a government role
- A client who finally finished writing a book and turned it into income

The IRS does not allow businesses created solely for tax advantages.

But many legitimate businesses start from existing skills or interests.

The bigger point is this:
The financial aid system defines income very narrowly.

Once you understand where AGI comes from, you may start to see opportunities to manage it more intentionally.

The Cost-of-Living Dilemma

Income plays a major role in your Student Aid Index (SAI).

And this is where things can start to feel…

unfair.

We live in Southern California.

If you're in places like New York, San Francisco, or Washington, D.C., you understand the feeling.

A $225,000 income might look strong on paper.

In reality, it can feel like you're just getting by.

Take that same income to a lower-cost area,
and it tells a completely different story.

The financial aid formula does not *meaningfully* adjust for the cost of living.

And that disconnect is real.

There is one important exception:

Under FAFSA rules, your **primary residence is not counted as an asset.**

So rising home values won't directly increase your SAI.

Still, the pressure is real.

The encouraging news?

We've seen many families make thoughtful adjustments—often with a CPA—that reduce AGI, improving both tax efficiency and financial aid positioning.

A common question is:
"Why didn't my CPA mention this before?"

As my husband, Dominic, likes to say:

"Because sometimes the juice isn't worth the squeeze."

Outside of college-planning years, small AGI adjustments may not matter much.

But during these years?

They can matter a lot.

Timing Matters

This is not something you want to figure out at the last minute.

By senior year, most key tax years are already locked in.

At that point, options are limited.

The families with the most flexibility usually begin planning for this during freshman or sophomore year.

This provides time for strategies to develop.

This is not something you rush.

What to Remember

- Financial aid income = **AGI**
- Below-the-line deductions don't affect aid
- Above-the-line deductions can
- Business owners often have more flexibility

- The formula doesn't fully reflect real-world cost-of-living differences
- Timing matters more than most families realize

Income is one piece of the puzzle.

The next one is just as important—and often more surprising:

Assets.

6

Assets

When I first sit down with families, most of their concerns center on income.

That makes sense.

But what often surprises parents is how much their assets can influence the outcome.

I'll hear something like:

"Wait… we were told to save in a 529, and now that hurts us? How is that fair?"

Even outside of 529 plans, many responsible families feel the same dilemma:

"We did the right things… and now it feels like we're being penalized for it."

To make sense of this, it helps to understand one key idea:

The financial aid system doesn't just measure how much you have.

It looks at where your money sits.

The easiest way to think about this is in categories—similar to how many families organize their finances:

- Retirement accounts
- Your home
- College savings plans
- Liquid savings and investments
- Business and real estate assets

Each of these is treated differently.

And those differences can have a meaningful impact on your outcome.

Let's start with retirement accounts.

Retirement Accounts

Numerous accounts fall under the retirement category.

Have you ever heard the fun fact that there are over 7,500 varieties of apples?

Well, now you have.

Retirement accounts are similar—there are many types, though most of us only recognize a handful.

The ones families typically know include:

- 401(k)
- Traditional IRA
- Roth IRA
- 403(b)
- SEP accounts
- Pensions

There are others—like KEOGHs and asset-backed pensions—but the crucial aspect to understand is how these accounts are treated in financial aid calculations.

Retirement Accounts & the FAFSA

Here's the good news.

When filling out the FAFSA, retirement accounts are not reported or counted in the asset calculation.

For many families, this is a relief—retirement savings are often their largest asset.

At every live workshop I host, I make a point of emphasizing this.

But when I later meet with some of those same families after they've submitted their FAFSA, I often observe something surprising.

You might have guessed it:

They included a retirement account.

To be fair, this mistake is easy to make.

The FAFSA instructions say you should not report retirement accounts; yet, they also ask about investments like mutual funds and stocks.

Since many retirement accounts contain those same investments, families sometimes accidentally list the entire balance.

In the past, this was usually simple to correct.

In recent years, correcting these mistakes has become much harder—especially after the first offer is issued.

So it's worth taking an extra moment to ensure retirement accounts are not included when completing the FAFSA.

Retirement Accounts & the CSS Profile

Remember the two applications we discussed earlier: the FAFSA and the CSS Profile.

Here's one of the first places where they diverge.

Many CSS Profile schools will ask you to disclose retirement account balances.

That sounds alarming, but it isn't always as bad as it seems.

Colleges generally understand the purpose of retirement accounts. They don't expect families to liquidate them to pay for college.

However, balances may still factor into the school's evaluation of your overall financial picture.

If your retirement accounts represent the majority of your wealth, the impact may be minimal.

But if you also have substantial assets outside of retirement accounts, the combined picture may influence how much aid a school offers.

Your Home

You saved.

You chose a good neighborhood.

Maybe you stretched a little to get into the best school district.

You made your payments — perhaps even some extra ones — and watched the value of your home rise.

Naturally, parents ask:

"How bad is this going to hurt us?"

As with retirement accounts, the answer depends on which application a school uses.

Your Home & the FAFSA

Under the FAFSA formula, your primary residence is not counted as an asset.

That's welcome news, especially for families living in areas where home values have increased significantly.

The good news is that the updated FAFSA form clarifies this, and mistakes here are now less common.

That wasn't always the case.

I have a personal story about this.

When I applied to college, my dad and I filled out the FAFSA together. We proudly included the value of my parents' home — which was paid off — along with my father's 401(k).

Want to guess how much financial aid I received?

Zero.

If we had understood how the system actually worked, the outcome could have been very different.

For me, it's not just "live and learn."

It's living and teaching others.

Your Home & the CSS Profile

The CSS Profile often tells a different story.

Many schools require families to report both the value of their home and the remaining mortgage balance.

Some institutions then apply what's referred to as a "home equity special assessment."

That means a portion of your home equity may be included in their calculation.

For example, if a home is worth $2 million and you owe $1.5 million, you have $500,000 in equity.

If a school applies a 5% assessment to that equity, it might add $25,000 to their estimate of your family's contribution toward college.

This doesn't automatically mean the school becomes unaffordable.

The full financial picture still matters.

Families with limited liquid assets may still receive substantial aid, even with home equity.

But it's important to understand that different schools treat home equity differently. This is another reason school selection plays such a significant role in the overall outcome.

College Savings Plans

This next bucket tends to generate the most debate.

I'm going to say something here that sometimes surprises parents:

I'm generally not a big fan of 529 plans when financial aid is a major concern.

That may sound surprising, since these plans are often promoted as the best way to save for college.

And to be fair, they do offer tax advantages.

But from a financial aid perspective, they don't always work the way families expect.

Why?

Because money saved in a 529 plan is specifically designated for college expenses.

From the school's perspective, those funds are already available to pay for college, thereby reducing the need for need-based aid.

Imagine a family with a modest income and very few assets aside from their retirement accounts and home.

Based on those factors alone, they might qualify for significant aid.

However, if that family has accumulated a large 529 balance over the years, the school may reasonably expect those funds to be used first.

I once worked with a family whose grandmother had opened a 529 account for their daughter at birth and contributed $5,000.

Through strong investment growth, that account eventually reached over $300,000.

That's incredible.

But it also meant the family's financial aid options were significantly impacted.

Some families are perfectly comfortable using those funds for college.

Others feel differently.

One father once told me:

"I know I can use it for college. But there's no guarantee my daughter will finish school or use the degree she chooses. I'd rather use that money for a down payment on her first house."

That's a personal decision every family must make.

Notably, the FAFSA and CSS Profile only ask about 529 plans owned by a member of the immediate household for the child's benefit.

The key takeaway is that 529 plans may influence financial aid outcomes more than many families realize.

If you already have a 529 plan with a modest balance, it's usually not a major concern.

But for larger balances, it can be worth discussing your options with a qualified advisor.

Liquid Savings & Investments

This category is often more straightforward.

These are the accounts many families hold at institutions like Bank of America, Charles Schwab, or Fidelity; they are not retirement accounts.

Examples include:

- savings accounts
- brokerage accounts
- taxable investments

These are the assets that financial aid formulas are most likely to notice.

The practical reality is simple:

If a family has substantial liquid assets, colleges will generally expect those funds to contribute toward the cost of education.

We once worked with a retired couple who had very little income but had inherited significant liquid assets.

Their Student Aid Index came in just under $600,000.

So yes — assets matter.

One important distinction to remember is that assets in a student's name are weighted much more heavily than assets held by the parents.

This reflects the assumption that parents need financial reserves for long-term stability, while students are expected to contribute a larger share of their own assets.

Business & Real Estate Assets

Your Business

Business assets were once among the most complicated aspects of the financial aid process.

In recent years, the rules have become somewhat simpler.

Under current FAFSA guidelines, businesses with fewer than 100 employees are generally not required to report their business assets.

That doesn't mean business owners should approach this casually.

Many business owners accidentally overreport assets.

A large balance in a business checking account, for example, may simply represent cash needed to cover payroll and operating expenses—not true business wealth.

If you own a business with multiple partners, complex ownership structures, or significant real estate holdings, it's often wise to seek professional guidance.

Small reporting mistakes can have meaningful consequences.

Additional Real Estate

Real estate other than your primary residence is generally considered an asset.

This includes rental properties, vacation homes, and commercial real estate.

When reporting property value, remember this:

Zillow is not the final authority.

Consider this: the founder of Zillow reportedly sold his house for 40% less than its Zestimate.

Online estimates can be helpful, but financial aid applications typically expect a reasonable estimate of the property's current market value, not an optimistic number pulled from a real estate website.

We know it's a great property.

You're proud of it.

Feel free to brag about it everywhere except the college applications.

A helpful way to think about this is to ask:

"What could this property realistically sell for if we needed to sell it soon?"

That perspective often produces a more realistic estimate.

This is not an uncommon approach. Even the IRS uses a formula called Quick Sale Value (QSV).

Just be prepared to support the value you report if a school requests clarification.

The Timing of Assets

Unlike income—which comes from tax returns filed long before college begins—assets are evaluated based on their value at the time you submit the financial aid application.

That might make it sound like you can move things around at the last minute.

Unfortunately, it rarely works that way.

Many of the strategies families use to position their assets take time to implement.

The more complex your financial picture, the earlier it makes sense to start thinking about these issues.

Final Thoughts on Assets

We covered a lot in this chapter.

One of Dominic's favorite reminders is:

"Not all assets are created equal when it comes to college."

Each school treats asset categories distinctly, and different schools apply those rules with their own variations.

Families with significant real estate or business interests often experience the biggest surprises here.

The good news is that once you understand how these categories work, you can begin to see how the type, location, and structure of your assets influence the outcome.

Next, we'll turn to the third gauge on our dashboard:

Timing.

7

Timing

I get a notification every time someone books an appointment on my calendar.

As part of the booking process, families answer a short questionnaire—including their student's high school year.

When I read "Senior," I'll be honest…

"Oh boy… I'm going to have to break some bad news."

What can we do to improve financial aid for a senior?

Very little—at least for the first year.

And nearly half the families I speak with find themselves in that position.

To be clear, there's no judgment in that.

Life happens.

We had one of our own children planning a path that didn't require college—until, not long before graduation, she changed direction.

Suddenly, a family that thought they had more time is staring at a very real financial reality and asking:

"Is there anything we can do?"

That's what this chapter is about.

Not perfection.

Not starting when your kids are toddlers.

Just understanding how timing actually works—so you can make better decisions from wherever you are today.

We'll break this into three parts:

- Income
- Assets
- The annual reset

Let's start with income.

Income Timing

I've touched on this before, but this is where it really clicks.

Your **Adjusted Gross Income (AGI)** is the basis for income in the financial aid system.

And it comes from the "**prior-prior year.**"

In plain terms:

If your student starts college in 2030, the FAFSA uses your **2028 tax return.**

Another way to think about it:

That income year typically covers:

- The second half of sophomore year
- The first half of junior year

Here's what that looks like:

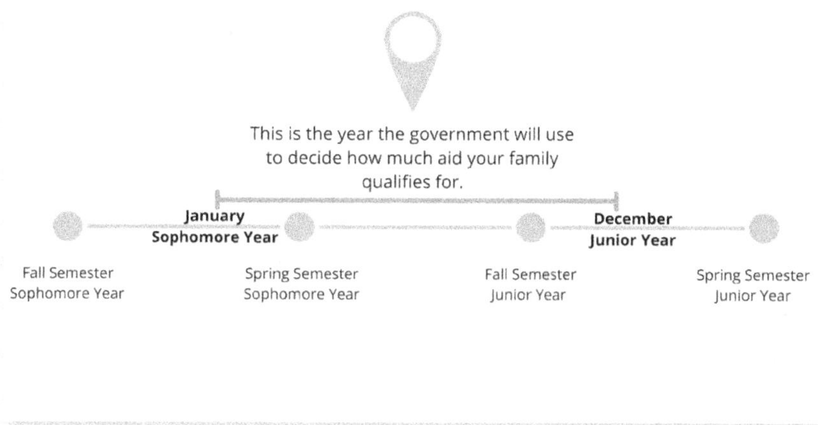

By the time senior year arrives…

That income year is already locked in.

Parents sometimes ask:
"Can we just amend the return?"

Technically, yes.

But most tax professionals will strongly discourage that approach—it can raise red flags and increase audit risk.

This is why we talk so much about starting in 9th or 10th grade.

By senior year, the most important income window has already passed.

Asset Timing

Assets work very differently.

Income is historical.

Assets are a snapshot.

They're measured based on their value **on the day you submit the FAFSA or CSS Profile.**

At first, that sounds like good news.

I often hear:

"Great—we still have time to fix the assets."

Sometimes.

But not as easily as it sounds.

As we discussed in the previous chapter, strategies around assets can include:

- Restructuring accounts
- Repositioning assets
- Adjusting how income flows through a business
- Preparing accurate property valuations

The key issue?

Those strategies take time.

They often involve coordination with a CPA, documentation, or structural changes that can't be done overnight.

So while assets are measured at a point in time...

The ability to influence them usually starts much earlier.

The Annual Reset

Now, let's say you planned.

Your student starts college.

You're done, right?

Not quite.

Financial aid recalculates every year.

You'll file a new FAFSA annually—and increasingly, the CSS Profile as well.

This leads some families to think:

"We'll fix it next year."

Sometimes you can.

But here's what I tell families:

"The first year sets the tone."

Once a financial aid office sees your financial picture, that picture becomes its reference point.

As someone on our team says:

"They can't unsee it."

If your AGI is $350,000 one year and drops to $110,000 the next year…

They're going to ask questions.

If a $1.5 million asset disappears…

They'll want to know why.

Even when changes are legitimate, the process becomes more complicated.

But if those numbers were never there to begin with?

The situation is often much simpler.

And that brings us back to the same theme you've seen throughout this book:

Earlier planning = more flexibility.

The Planning Timeline

Before we walk through a typical timeline, one quick note:

Some families need to start earlier due to complexity.

Examples include:

- Divorce with financially strong parents
- Remarriage with significant income/assets
- Large real estate portfolios
- Complex business ownership
- Estranged parents with financial resources
- Household income above ~$500,000

In those cases, earlier planning is even more important.

For most families, though, this general timeline works well:

9th Grade

Early awareness.

- Understand state aid programs.
- Begin conversations if income or assets are already high.

Sophomore Year

The planning window.

- Begin implementing income strategies.
- Consider formalizing side businesses or consulting.

Junior Year

The key income window closes.

- By winter break, the income window is set.
- Strategies should already be in place.

Senior Year

Application phase.

- Most financial variables are already determined.
- Limited room for adjustment.

The Funnel

I often describe this as a funnel.

Early on, it's wide:

Options. Flexibility. Time.

Each year, it narrows.

By senior year?

It's tight.

That's when families feel the pressure.

So yes—the earlier you start, the better.

But if you didn't start early?

You're not alone.

And you're not out of options—you just need to understand where you are in the funnel.

Where We Are So Far

At this point, you've seen how three key factors interact:

- Income
- Assets
- Timing

And hopefully, something is starting to shift.

It's beginning to feel less random.

Less frustrating. Less… unfair.

There's one more factor that can dramatically change the outcome:

School selection.

And that's where we're going next.

8

School Selection

In earlier chapters, I mentioned that many families believe income is the main factor determining financial aid.

As you've now seen, income matters.

But it is only one part of the picture.

In this chapter, we're going to talk about what may ultimately be the most important factor of all:

School selection.

After learning about the FAFSA and the Student Aid Index, many families assume the FAFSA—and by extension, the government—decides what they will pay for college.

That's not quite right.

The FAFSA calculates a number.
The school decides what to do with it.

Your SAI helps determine your financial need. But the school's philosophy, budget, and priorities determine how much of that need they will actually meet.

To understand that, we need to briefly revisit the concept of need.

Need

Earlier, we introduced the basic formula:

Cost of Attendance – SAI = Demonstrated Need

In plain English, your "need" is calculated only after your SAI has already been determined.

As a parent, I know how I might define need:
"I need help paying for college so I don't go broke."

The financial aid system defines it differently.

Instead, it uses the formula.

Once that number is calculated, the real question becomes:

How much of that need will this school choose to meet?

And that answer varies significantly from one institution to another.

Need-Based vs. Merit-Based

Most financial aid falls into two broad categories.

Need-based aid helps offset the gap created by the formula we just discussed.

Merit-based aid is awarded for academic achievements, leadership, athletics, talent, or other accomplishments.

But here's something many families overlook:

Need even influences merit aid.

For example, imagine two students competing for the same scholarship.

Both have a 4.0 GPA.

Both have similar extracurricular activities.
Both are strong applicants.

One student's family has demonstrated a need of $70,000.

The other has demonstrated a need of $10,000.

All else being equal, **a school may prioritize the student whose family has greater need.**

Why does that matter?

Because even if your income and assets are too high to qualify for significant amounts of traditional need-based aid, lowering your SAI can still be important.

In competitive situations, it may influence how merit awards are distributed.

That's why school selection is so crucial.

Once need is calculated, the school decides how generous it wants or needs to be.

Seller & Buyer Schools

You may be familiar with the terms "buyer's market" and "seller's market" in real estate.

In a buyer's market, buyers have leverage, and sellers may need to negotiate.

In a seller's market, demand is high, allowing sellers to command top dollar.

The same concept applies to colleges.

Some schools have students competing to attend, while other schools are competing to attract students.

Where a school falls on that spectrum can significantly impact financial aid.

This is not an all-or-nothing classification.

It's a continuum.

Some schools are strong seller schools, while others are strong buyer schools. Many fall somewhere in between.

Let's start with seller schools.

Seller Schools

Seller schools have more applicants than they can reasonably admit.

Demand is high.

As a result, they do not always need to offer large financial incentives to attract students.

When students are eager to attend, and families are willing to pay, these schools can reallocate resources to other priorities: research, facilities, faculty, programs, or long-term institutional goals.

Examples of schools that often behave like seller schools include:

- New York University
- Stanford University
- UCLA
- University of Michigan
- University of Texas at Austin

These are well-known, academically strong, and popular with students.

Many also attract large numbers of international applicants. Since financial aid for international students is often limited, many of those families pay full price.

One important note:
These categories can shift.

A school that behaves like a seller school one year may become more generous the next year, depending on enrollment goals, leadership decisions, or changes in demand.

Generally, seller schools tend to offer less aggressive financial aid packages.

That does not mean they *never* offer aid.

Highly desirable students can still receive strong packages.

Broadly speaking, these schools do not need to use aid as aggressively to attract students.

Buyer Schools

Buyer schools are typically smaller private universities or lesser-known public institutions.

This does not mean they are inferior schools.

In fact, many offer excellent academic programs.

However, they may be located in smaller cities, have fewer students, or lack the name recognition of larger universities.

For this reason, these schools must compete for students, and one of the most effective ways to compete is through financial aid.

These schools often offer generous merit awards, substantial need-based aid, or a combination of both to attract strong applicants.

Many families are surprised to discover that a smaller private university may ultimately cost far less than a well-known public university.

The graph below illustrates this idea.

Schools on the buyer side of the spectrum tend to offer more aid, while those on the seller side often offer less.

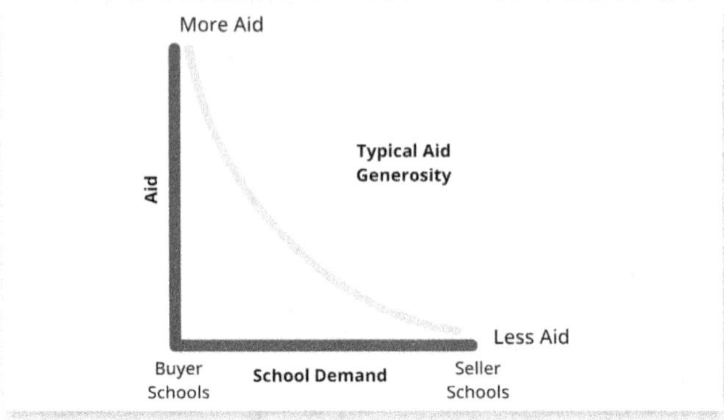

Think of colleges as existing on a spectrum between buyer schools and seller schools.

How Do You Tell?

So how can you estimate where a school falls on the spectrum?

Professionals in this field often use specialized tools and databases to analyze institutional aid policies.

However, you can still find useful information on your own.

Here are three ways to start.

Ask Them

It always surprises me how many families hesitate to call a financial aid office.

You absolutely can.

In fact, schools are often happy to answer thoughtful questions from prospective families.

Here are three questions I recommend asking every school you are seriously considering:

1. **What percentage of demonstrated financial need do you meet on average?** This tells you how much of the gap the school typically covers.

2. **Of the aid you offer, how much is free money versus loans?** A school that meets 50% of need with half of its aid as loans may be far less generous than a school that meets 80% of need, mostly with grants.

3. **What is the average time to graduate?** This question is often overlooked. Paying for four years of college is very different from paying for five or six.

Look at Acceptance Rates

You may already be familiar with schools being classified as likely, target, reach, and high reach.

A rough framework looks like this:

- **Likely:** 60–80%+ acceptance rate
- **Target:** 30–60%
- **Reach:** 15–30%
- **High reach:** Under 15%

This is not a perfect science.

However, schools with lower acceptance rates often behave more like seller schools.

Schools with higher acceptance rates may be competing harder for students.

Acceptance rate should not be the only factor you consider.

But when used alongside the other research we've discussed, it can be a helpful signal.

Endowments

Another factor that can influence financial aid is a school's endowment.

An endowment is essentially a large investment fund built over time through donations, alumni gifts, and investment returns.

Many well-known universities have endowments worth billions of dollars.

However, schools typically do not spend the endowment itself.

They invest it and spend a percentage of annual earnings — often around 4–5% per year.

Those earnings may fund things like:

- Research
- Faculty positions
- Facilities
- Scholarships and financial aid

A larger endowment can give a school greater capacity to offer generous aid.

But capacity is not the same as willingness.

Some endowment funds are restricted by donors for specific purposes, limiting the schools' use of those assets.

And some wealthy schools still behave like schools with limited resources because demand is so strong.

The takeaway is simple:

A large endowment may indicate that a school has money.

It does not automatically mean it will allocate more of it to your family.

School Selection & Strategy

Every school has a finite financial aid budget.

Lowering your income or repositioning assets to reduce your SAI can absolutely improve your financial aid situation.

But choosing the right schools can be just as important.

Dominic often says something in our workshops that I always tease him about.

So I can't believe I'm including it in the book.

But he's right.

> You can't borrow money from your broke friends.
>
> So don't try to get money from a school that isn't giving any.

I'll never hear the end of including that quote.

But the point stands.

School selection is one of the most powerful — and most overlooked — factors determining how much financial aid a family ultimately receives.

9

What to Remember About the System

Now you've seen the four main gauges that shape financial aid outcomes:

Income

What the system believes your family earns, and when that income is measured.

Assets

Where your money is held, how it is titled, and how the FAFSA or CSS Profile treats it.

Timing

When income and assets appear in the formulas, and how early planning creates more flexibility.

School selection

Which schools your student applies to, how those schools distribute aid, and whether they have both the ability and willingness to help.

These four factors work together.

That is why two families with similar incomes, similar homes, and similar lifestyles can receive very different offers.

And this is why understanding the system is so important:

You can stop relying on assumptions and start making strategic decisions.

But even when families understand the mechanics, many still make decisions based on beliefs that simply aren't true.

In the next section, we'll walk through some of the most common assumptions families make about paying for college—and why those assumptions often lead to paying far more than necessary.

PART III

The Costly Assumptions

I meet with families every week who have done extensive research on college aid.

They've attended online workshops,
joined Facebook groups,
listened to guidance counselors,
and talked to friends, neighbors, and other parents who have already been through the process.

The problem isn't that they haven't tried to learn.

They have.

The problem is that much of the information they hear is either outdated, incomplete, misunderstood, or repeated so often that it starts to sound like fact.

Sometimes it comes from a rule that used to be true.

Sometimes it comes from a small misunderstanding of how a school applies its policy.

And sometimes it comes from a well-meaning neighbor who confidently describes a situation that may have little to do with yours.

Whatever the source, many families enter this process with assumptions about how financial aid works.

Some of those assumptions can be costly.

They can cause families to miss opportunities, eliminate good schools too early, skip important forms, or pay thousands more than necessary.

In this section, we're going to walk through the assumptions I hear most often.

Some may contradict what you've heard, even from those who should know.

Don't blame them.

The college aid system changes frequently, and the details can be hard to keep up with.

I live and breathe this every day, so I have a front-row seat to what's really happening.

This section matters because no matter how good your strategy is, if you begin with the wrong assumptions, you can still end up heading in the wrong direction.

10

"Private Schools Are Too Expensive"

When I meet with families and review their initial college list, one thing often stands out:

There are no private schools on it.

When I ask why, the answer is almost always the same.

"They're too expensive."

On paper, that conclusion seems reasonable.

A private university like Loyola Marymount might approach $100,000 per year, while an in-state public university like UC Santa Barbara might be closer to $30,000.

That looks like simple math.

Public universities receive state subsidies.

They enroll far more students.

Their published tuition prices are lower.

And for many parents, that's exactly how college pricing worked when they were students.

But today, that assumption can cost families tens of thousands of dollars.

One of the biggest misconceptions about college pricing is that the school simply sets a price and financial aid reduces it.

In reality, many colleges work backward.

They decide how much they want a student to pay, then build a financial aid package to match that number.

That's why the same student can receive dramatically different offers from different schools.

Let's break down why.

Financial Aid

Think back to the last time you bought a car.

You walked onto the lot and found one you liked. Maybe even one you loved.

Then you looked at the sticker on the window.

What was your first thought?

Probably something like:

"There's no way I'm paying that."

Then the negotiation began.

In the car world, a simple rule applies:

Sticker price does not equal the price you actually pay.

Something similar happens in the college world.

And unlike negotiating at a dealership, you don't have to pretend to walk out of the financial aid office three times to get a better deal.

We discussed some of these factors in the previous chapter.

Private schools often have larger financial aid budgets than public universities.

Many have endowments that help fund scholarships and grants.

Some are "buyer" schools—institutions that actively use financial aid to attract students.

All of these factors can lead private universities to approach financial aid very differently from many public schools.

To see how this works, let's look at a simplified example.

The Tale of Two Schools

Before we look at how financial aid changes the outcome, let's revisit the formula:

Cost of Attendance – Student Aid Index = Demonstrated Need

The Cost of Attendance varies from school to school.

Your Student Aid Index does not.

Now let's compare two hypothetical schools:

Public School		Private School
$30,000	**Cost of Attendance**	$70,000
— $20,000	**SAI**	— $20,000
$10,000	**Need**	$50,000

At first glance, the public school still looks like the obvious choice.

But this is where institutional aid policy changes everything.

The Impact of Financial Aid

Earlier, I introduced three important questions families should ask every school:

- How much demonstrated need does the school meet?
- How much of that aid is money that does not need to be repaid?
- How long does it typically take students to graduate?

This is where those questions start to matter.

Let's use common averages for this example:

	Public School	Private School
Need Met	50%	92%
Gift Aid Portion	50%	100%

Now let's apply those numbers:

	Public School	Private School
Cost of Attendance	$30,000	$70,000
Student Aid Index	$20,000	$20,000
Demonstrated Need	$10,000	$50,000
Need Met	$5,000	$46,000
Gift Aid	$2,500	$46,000
Loan/Self-help Portion	$2,500	$0
Estimated Yearly Cost	**$27,500**	**$24,000**

Hold the presses.

Are we saying the more expensive school is the cheaper option?

Sometimes, yes.

And this is not uncommon.

But there is one more factor families often overlook.

Graduation Time

Before we move forward, let me address a question that often comes up during our workshops.

"Why would a public school take six years? That doesn't sound right."

First, this is not a criticism of public universities.

There are exceptional public schools across the country. I attended one myself, as did Dominic's sister; our own daughter is currently attending one.

But several structural factors can contribute to longer average graduation timelines at large public universities:

Impacted classes

Large student populations can make it harder to secure required courses.

Less individualized advising

Students may change majors, retake classes, or struggle to receive timely guidance.

Budget constraints

Some public universities simply do not have the resources to provide the same level of student support as smaller institutions.

None of this guarantees a six-year timeline.

Many students graduate in four years.

But when evaluating the total cost of a degree, average time to graduation matters.

Let's include that in our example:

Public School		Private School
6 Years	Years to Graduate	4 Years
$27,500	Yearly Cost	$24,000
$165,000	**Total Education Cost**	**$96,000**

This represents a significant difference for the school that initially looked "more expensive."

Student Examples

This kind of outcome is not uncommon.

A few years ago, we helped a single father in California who had identical twin daughters.

Not only did they look alike, but they had similar grades and comparable test scores.

However, they had very different ideas about college.

One wanted to stay in California and attend a public university.

The other wanted to leave the state and attend a private school.

Because of in-state tuition, their father felt comfortable with the public school option, but he was worried about the private school.

When the financial aid packages arrived, he called me, pleasantly surprised.

One daughter attended UC Berkeley, one of the most respected public universities in the country.

The other attended Emory University, a highly regarded private university in Georgia.

On paper, Berkeley looked like the more affordable option.

Emory appeared impossibly expensive.

But when the numbers came in, he said:

> "Ivana, I can't believe it. Emory is almost half the cost of Berkeley."

The Goal

The point of sharing examples like this is not to suggest that private schools are always cheaper.

They are not.

Sometimes, public universities are absolutely the best financial option.

The real takeaway is this:

Do not eliminate schools based solely on the published price.

Build a list based on:

- Academic fit
- Personal fit
- Financial aid potential

A school that seems expensive at first glance may ultimately cost less.

And you don't want your student to miss out on a school that might be a great fit simply because the sticker price scared you away.

The Next Assumption

After hearing examples like this, many parents have the same reaction:

"That's interesting... but we probably earn too much to qualify for financial aid anyway."

This belief is incredibly common.

And in the next chapter, we're going to explore why it can also be a costly assumption.

11

"We Make Too Much"

At our live events, I regularly have parents approach me afterward and express a similar sentiment: *"The information was great... but I'm sure we make too much to qualify."*

I love this topic because it gives me the chance to challenge one of the most expensive myths in college planning:

High income does not automatically mean no financial aid.

Why the Myth Exists

One reason families believe this is simple:

They've heard it from someone else.

Friends.
Family.
School counselors.
"Experts."

There is a widespread belief that **high income = no financial aid.**

To be fair, that can be true in some situations.

But it is far from the whole story.

As we've discussed throughout this book, multiple factors influence financial aid. Income matters, but it's not the only factor.

School selection matters.
Assets matter.
Timing matters.
Institutional policy matters.

So, regardless of what you've heard, you may still qualify for aid even with a high income.

Another major reason this myth persists is that many families define financial aid too narrowly.

Usually, they are thinking about one specific program: The Pell Grant.

The Pell Grant

If you attended college in the 90s or early 2000s, the Pell Grant was often the primary form of aid people recognized.

The Pell Grant is a federal program that has been around since the 1970s. It was named after Senator Claiborne Pell and designed to help lower-income families pay for college.

For many years, eligibility was based largely on income.

Today, your Student Aid Index, or SAI, includes both income and assets.

The Pell Grant operates on a sliding scale.

As of 2025, the maximum award is $7,395. Families with an SAI of 0 or lower may qualify for the maximum award. The award then decreases as SAI rises, eventually phasing out.

Crystal clear, right?

Below is an image illustrating this using numbers that reflect the rule change.

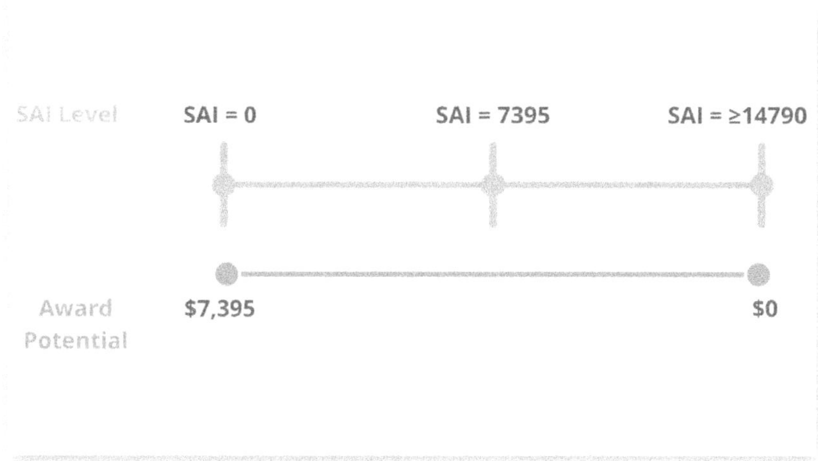

The important takeaway is simple:

The Pell Grant is still primarily designed for lower-income families.

Where the Confusion Begins

This is where many families get stuck.

They use Pell Grant eligibility as their definition of financial aid.

So when they realize they won't qualify for a Pell Grant, they assume they won't qualify for anything.

But Pell Grants are only one piece of the financial aid system.

And for many families, they are not the most important piece.

A maximum Pell Grant may help.

But it will not cover the cost of a $90,000 school.

In other words:

There is a lot of other money out there.

Sources of Aid

I encourage families to think of financial aid in layers.

First, the federal government reviews your FAFSA.

That may also trigger state aid, depending on where you live.

Then comes institutional aid — money offered directly by the colleges themselves.

Finally, there are scholarships, both institutional and private.

It looks something like this:

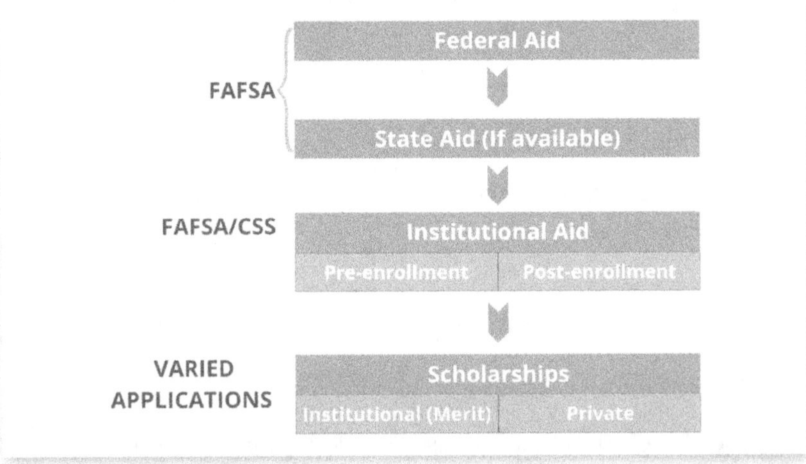

Where the Money Actually Comes From

The order in which aid is evaluated does not always reflect where the largest amounts of aid come from.

For many families, the largest opportunity is not federal aid.

The typical order looks like this:

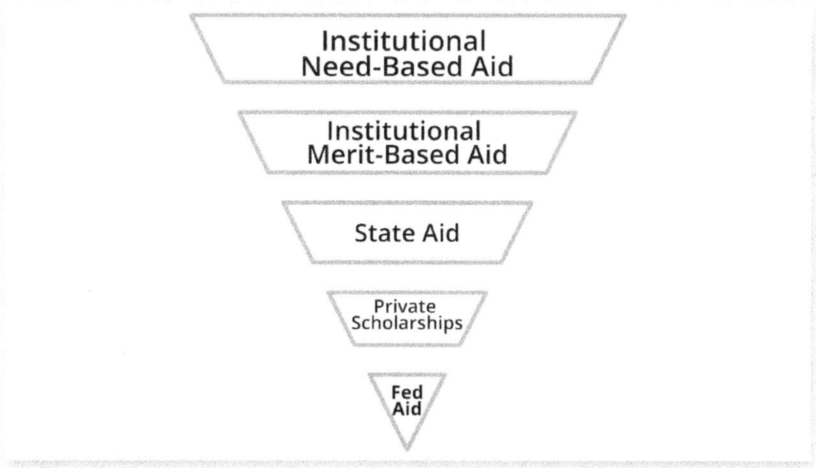

Institutional aid often provides the largest contribution to college costs.

That means money from the school itself.

And this brings us back to a key idea from the previous chapter:

Not all schools treat financial aid the same way.

Some schools have more money.
Some schools are more willing to use it.
Some schools use aid aggressively to attract students.

That is why school selection matters so much.

We will discuss school selection in much more detail in an upcoming chapter.

Pre-Enrollment & Post-Enrollment Aid

This next concept is important, and many families miss it.

Most families focus on pre-enrollment aid.

That's the money listed on the financial aid offer letter before the student decides where to attend.

That makes sense.

Those numbers matter.

But there is another category:

Post-enrollment aid.

This is money students can access after they are admitted or enrolled, often through the school's internal systems or student portal.

Depending on the school, this may include scholarships from:

- Academic departments
- Alumni-funded programs
- Internal university initiatives
- Major-specific opportunities

These awards are often smaller.

But they can add up.

And because many families never look for them, the applicant pool can be much smaller.

Even better, these scholarships are often not tied directly to family income or assets.

A Real Example

We had a student a few years ago who was not a U.S. citizen.

That matters because aid is often very limited for non-citizens.

She was accepted into USC's film studies program.

USC did not offer her institutional aid.

Initially, attending USC looked like a very expensive decision. Then something unexpected happened.

Around the same time, a USC film studies alum's movie became a hit, and its success created a significant tax situation.

And USC is very good at helping alumni solve tax problems through charitable giving.

The alumnus made a substantial donation specifically to the film studies department.

As a result, our student secured $20,000 per year in departmental funding after enrolling.

That money had nothing to do with the financial aid office or USC's standard aid policies.

And it had nothing to do with the family's income.

Income Isn't the Real Question

When people say, "You won't qualify," they are often unknowingly referring to federal aid—usually the Pell Grant.

But for many families, that is not where the biggest opportunity lies.

The bigger opportunity often comes from the schools themselves.

Especially schools that have the resources and motivation to attract students.

We routinely work with families earning well into the six figures who still receive meaningful aid.

For example:

- A family earning over $300,000 received $30,000 per year from USC.
- A single mom earning over $200,000 received more than $48,000 per year from Hamilton.
- Multiple high-income families received discounts of 50% or more on the cost of attendance at LMU.

Financial aid is not a yes-or-no question. It's a spectrum.

The Real Takeaway

Don't assume you won't qualify simply because your income is high.

That assumption can cause you to eliminate opportunities before you even understand what is possible.

The question is not:
"Do we qualify for aid?"

The better question is:
"Which schools are most likely to offer it?"

The Next Assumption

This belief often leads directly into the next one:

"There's no point in filling out the FAFSA."

And that can be an even more costly mistake.

12

"There Is No Point in Filling Out the FAFSA"

When I meet a family for the first time, I often hear this:

"I don't think we're going to bother filling out the FAFSA."

When I ask why, the answers are almost always the same.

The Four Reasons People Skip the FAFSA

"We make (or have) too much, so what's the point?"
"It's too much work."
"I think we missed the deadline."
"It can hurt your admission chances."

If you've thought any of those, you're not alone.

But like the assumptions we've already covered, this one can cost you — especially when you might need help the most.

Studies suggest that nearly 80% of families make mistakes on financial aid forms.

The number one mistake?

Not filing them at all.

Since you might be curious:

- Number two: overreporting assets.
- Number three: mistakes involving divorce or custody.

We'll cover those later.

For now, let's focus on the FAFSA.

The FAFSA Misconception

Most families think of the FAFSA as:

"The form you fill out to get financial aid."

That's true.

But here's the mistake:

"If we won't qualify, there's no reason to fill it out."

That belief usually comes back to the Pell Grant.

If you don't qualify for Pell, it feels like you don't qualify for anything.

But as you've seen, the Pell Grant is only one piece of the system.

At many schools, the FAFSA **triggers access to institutional aid** — the money that actually moves the needle.

And if you don't file it?

You're simply not considered.

That alone should get your attention.

But there's an even more important way to think about it.

The FAFSA is Free Insurance

Yes — insurance.

Not because it guarantees you aid today.

But because it protects you if something changes tomorrow.

And I know what you're thinking:

"That won't happen to us."

I hear that all the time.

The Reality Most Families Don't Plan For

The National Association of Student Financial Aid Administrators (NASFAA) shares a statistic that surprises almost every parent:

> **About one-third of students experience a significant financial disruption during college.**

One-third.

Think about that.

Roughly 15 million students start college each year.

That means around 5 million families will face a change that negatively impacts their ability to pay.

What causes it?

- Job loss
- Business downturns
- Health issues
- Divorce
- Unexpected expenses

In other words:

"Life."

And while I sincerely hope nothing like that happens to your family…

Wouldn't you rather be prepared?

The Cost of Inaction

In the financial aid world, these situations are called **"changes in circumstances."**

Here's what most families don't realize:
If you don't have a FAFSA on file, many schools won't consider you for need-based aid — even if your situation changes.

You don't get to go back and opt in later.

And when that door is closed…

Your options become very limited.

Real-World Examples

Let me show you what this looks like in real life.

Sole-Income Dad

We worked with a family where the father was the sole income earner.

He was well-compensated and strong, working a physically demanding job.

His daughter was about to start her first semester — the first in the family to go to college.

One morning, he didn't feel great.

He went to work anyway.

That night, he felt worse and went straight to bed.

The next morning, he went to the doctor.

The doctor told him:

"I can't help you here. You need to go to the ER."

At the hospital, he slipped into a coma.

He was out for six weeks.

Out of work for six months.

The family had already paid for the first semester.

But what about the second?

Even though his income would normally disqualify them from aid, they had one important thing in place:

A FAFSA.

His daughter went to the financial aid office and explained what happened.

Because they had filed, the school was able to step in.

They provided enough support to cover the next semester.

The only reason that was possible?

They had a FAFSA on file.

A form that initially produced little to no aid…

Ended up acting exactly like insurance when they needed it most.

Thankfully, he made a full recovery.

But that situation changed overnight.

"That's Extreme…"

Fair.

Let me give you another.

Successful Family

I've changed a few identifying details here, but the situation is very real.

We worked with a family where one parent was in healthcare, and the other had a strong corporate career.

They had a full house and a busy life—private schools, sports, all of it.

Around the holidays, everything changed quickly.

What started as a routine medical appointment turned into more testing…

And then a diagnosis no one wants to hear.

Soon after, treatment began.

Work stopped.

And as if that wasn't enough, the other parent lost their job shortly after.

They went from financially comfortable…
to trying to figure out how to keep everything together, including college.

And then the next student was right behind, with college just around the corner.

But they had one thing working in their favor:

They had a FAFSA on file.

Despite their income and assets, we had completed it.

The school reviewed the change in circumstances and stepped in to help.

Because they could.

No FAFSA = very few options
FAFSA filed = options

Why This Matters

These situations are not rare.

In a single year, we've seen:

- Cancer diagnoses
- A parent passing away
- Wildfires destroying homes
- Families losing utilities due to natural disasters
- Divorces and separations

And that's not a complete list.

In that same admissions cycle, we also saw serious health issues, extended hospitalizations, and multiple families navigating major life changes all at once.

At some point, Dominic and I started saying the same thing to each other:

That one-third statistic might actually be low.

Life simply doesn't stay static for four years.

Every one of those families had one thing in common:

They had a FAFSA on file.

And because of that…
they had options when they needed them most.

The Four Objections (Revisited)

Let's go back to the reasons families skip the FAFSA.

"We won't qualify."

That's not the point.

This is about keeping doors open.

And none of the strategy in this book matters if you don't file.

"It's too much work."

It used to be.

It was a mess.

It's not nearly as bad anymore.

And compared to the cost of college?

This is one of the highest-return uses of your time.

"We missed it."

If your student isn't a senior yet, you didn't miss anything.

Did you miss it?

Call the financial aid office.

There is often more flexibility than people realize.

"It hurts admissions."

This one has gained traction recently.

Most schools are need-blind, meaning your financial situation does not impact admissions decisions.

Schools that are need-aware typically require additional forms, such as the CSS Profile.

The FAFSA itself plays little to no role in admissions.

And even if it did…

The upside of filing far outweighs the risk.

A Word About the CSS Profile

Some schools list the CSS Profile as "optional."

But if you read closely, it's only optional if you don't intend to apply for financial aid.

If you are willing to pay full price, you can skip it.

But if you're reading this book…

That's probably not your plan.

In most cases, you should complete it.

The Real Takeaway

Dominic likes to joke that my FAFSA "rant" is his favorite part of our workshop.

He's probably right.

Because we've seen too many families **skip this step and regret it later.**

So here's what I want you to remember:

Filing the FAFSA is not about whether you think you'll qualify.

It's about keeping doors open, preserving flexibility, and protecting your family from the unknown.

The Next Assumption

We've now addressed two of the biggest misconceptions:

"We make too much."

"There's no point in filling out the FAFSA."

But there's another assumption that limits families:

"Out-of-state schools are too expensive."

Let's tackle that next.

13

"Out-of-State Schools Are Too Expensive"

Ironically, I could just as easily title this chapter:
"Out-of-State Schools Are Cheaper."

Because I hear both.

And here's the truth:

They're both wrong.

And they're both right.

Which is part of what makes this process so confusing.

The good news?

Once you understand what's actually driving the cost, it becomes much easier to navigate.

What "Out-of-State" Actually Means

When most families talk about "out-of-state pricing," they're really talking about public universities.

Public schools are funded, in part, by state tax dollars.

So they prioritize:

- In-state students
- Students who are more likely to stay and contribute to the state economy

To make that work, they charge out-of-state students more.

Sometimes significantly more.

That's where the assumption comes from.

The First Big Miss

Here's what most families don't realize:

That concept doesn't apply the same way to private schools.

Private universities typically don't have meaningful price differences between in-state and out-of-state students.

Which means:

There is typically no built-in penalty for geography.

That alone changes the conversation.

Where the Confusion Starts

Now let's look at the numbers most families see:

- In-state public: $30,000
- Out-of-state public: $50,000
- Private school: $70,000

At first glance, this feels obvious.

In-state wins.

Case closed.

And on paper… that's true.

But as you've seen throughout this book:

Sticker price is not the final price.

The Other Side of the Confusion

Sometimes I hear the opposite:

"Out-of-state is way cheaper."

That usually comes from seeing a low tuition number online.

Something like:

"Wait… this school is only $8,000?"

But that's typically tuition only.

Once you add:

- Housing
- Food
- Fees
- Travel

The number looks very different.

So now we have two competing assumptions:
Out-of-state is too expensive.
Out-of-state is a bargain.

Incomplete information is the basis for both assumptions.

So Which One Is It?

More expensive or cheaper?

The real answer is:
It depends on how the school behaves.

Not the state.

Not the label of public vs. private.

The internal strategy of the school.

Buyer vs. Seller (Quick Reminder)

Some schools are trying to attract students.

Some don't have to.

Buyer schools:

- Compete for students
- Offer more aid
- Are often private (but not always)

Seller schools:

- Have more demand than seats
- Offer less aid
- Can charge full price

And here's the key connection:

Many buyer schools are out-of-state private schools.

Why This Matters

Your in-state public university?

They already have demand.

They don't need to offer large discounts.

But an out-of-state school—especially one trying to grow or compete nationally—may offer:

- Larger grants
- More flexibility

- More aggressive pricing

To get your student to say yes.

Now Let's Revisit the Math

Same example:

- In-state public: $30,000
- Out-of-state public: $50,000
- Private school: $70,000

Still looks like in-state is the best option.

But what if:

- The private school offers $50,000 in aid
- Or the out-of-state public offers $25,000 in incentives
- Or they waive out-of-state tuition altogether

Now what?

The math changes.

Sometimes dramatically.

Real Examples

You've already seen one example earlier:

The identical twins.

One attended Berkeley.

The other attended Emory.

On paper, Berkeley looked like the affordable option.

In reality, Emory—the private, out-of-state school—cost significantly less.

And it's not just private schools.

We had a strong student from Texas this year, with nothing unusual on paper.

She received a very generous offer from the University of Arkansas, an out-of-state public school.

When we compared the numbers, Arkansas was more affordable than her in-state options.

Why?

They were in **buyer mode.**

The Reality Check

This doesn't mean:
Out-of-state is always cheaper
Private is always better
Public schools are a bad choice

It means:

You can't make the decision based on sticker price alone.

What You Should Do Instead

When building your school list:
Start with fit.
Then evaluate cost.

Not the other way around.

Because if you eliminate schools too early based on assumptions…

You may never see what was possible.

The Real Takeaway

I say this a lot, and it applies here just as much:

The costs are rarely what they appear to be at first.

College pricing may not feel logical.

But it is predictable—once you know what to look for.

The Next Step

Once families start to understand this, the next question usually becomes:

"Okay… we may just have to rely on scholarships."

And that brings us to the next assumption.

14

"They'll Get Scholarships"

I often hear families—especially those with strong students or student-athletes—say something like:

"We're not too worried. I'm sure they'll get some scholarships."

And I understand why that feels like a plan.

Your student works hard.
Scholarships are "free money."
There is no repayment.

And we've all heard stories of students landing big awards.

It sounds like the solution.

The problem is…

For most families, it's not a strategy.

Why This Feels True

Scholarships are one of the most talked-about parts of the college process.

Friends mention them.

Schools promote them.

Students hear about them constantly.

And occasionally, you hear about someone who gets a big one.

A full ride.

A major award.

That story resonates.

Especially when you're thinking:

"My student is just as strong—if not stronger."

So naturally, families start to think:

"That's what we'll do."

But those stories are not the norm.

The Scholarship Reality

Scholarships absolutely exist.

And they can help.

But there are a few realities most families don't see at the beginning:
They are competitive.
They often require time, essays, and organization.
And many of them are relatively small.

It's very common to see scholarships in the $500 to $2,000 range.

Helpful? Yes.

If you win several, they can add up.

But are they game-changing on their own?

Usually not.

Scholarship Stacking

This is where things get more nuanced—and more important.

You may hear the term **"scholarship stacking."**

It means exactly what it sounds like:

Adding scholarships together to build a larger financial aid package.

Some schools allow this.

Others don't.

Instead, they use something called **scholarship displacement.**

Here's what that looks like:

You receive a $20,000 grant from the school.
You win a $2,500 private scholarship.

If stacking is allowed:
→ Your total aid becomes $22,500.

If the school uses displacement:
→ The school reduces its aid.
→ You still end up at $20,000 total.

Same scholarship.

A very different outcome.

This is why understanding a school's policy matters because it directly impacts how valuable those scholarships actually are.

The good news?

In some cases, we've been able to negotiate partial stacking—even at schools that don't typically allow it.

But it's not something you want to assume.

The Time Trade-Off

There's another piece families often overlook:

Scholarships take time.

Time to search.
Time to apply.
Time to write essays.

And that time has to come from somewhere.

Usually, it competes with:

- Schoolwork
- Extracurricular activities
- The college application process itself

So the real question becomes:

Where is your student's time best spent?

While scholarships can help…

They are not the only—or even the primary—source of funding for most families.

Where the "Big Money" Comes From

As we've discussed throughout this book, the largest sources of funding typically come from:

The schools themselves.
Institutional grants.
Strategic school selection.

—not outside scholarships.

That doesn't mean scholarships don't matter.

They do.

They're just not the foundation.

What About Full-Ride Scholarships?

This is where expectations can really diverge.

Families often say:

"We're hoping for a full ride."

And I get it.

That's the story we hear.

But in reality, full-ride scholarships are rare.

Even strong students often receive partial awards.

This is especially important for student-athletes.

There's a common assumption that athletics will cover most—or all—of the cost.

Sometimes it does.

More often, it doesn't.

Many sports don't offer full scholarships to every athlete.

Instead, coaches divide their scholarship budgets across multiple players.

And even when a student receives a strong offer, it's not always guaranteed for four years.

We've seen situations where:

- Scholarships adjust after the first year.
- Playing time impacts future aid.
- Injuries change everything.

In one case, we worked with a student who had a volleyball opportunity lined up—until she tore her ACL during her senior year.

The scholarship disappeared.

That's not to say these opportunities aren't valuable.

They absolutely are.

But relying on them as the primary plan introduces a level of uncertainty that most families don't recognize upfront.

A Better Way to Think About It

The best way to view scholarships is as:

a supplement
a bonus
a way to reduce costs further

—not the foundation of your plan.

If scholarships materialize, they should enhance a good plan—

not rescue a weak one.

Other "Free Money" to Consider

There are also ways students can reduce costs over time:

Work-study programs
Resident advisor (RA) roles
Teaching assistant (TA) opportunities
Department-based awards

These can absolutely help—especially after enrollment.

They may not be the primary solution either, but they can add up.

And they come with the added benefit of building real-world skills.

We'll break these down further in the strategy section.

The Takeaway

If your plan is:

"We'll just figure it out with scholarships."

I'd strongly encourage you to rethink that approach.

Scholarships can play a role.

But they shouldn't be the strategy.

Once families realize scholarships aren't the entire answer, the next thought is usually:

"Okay… what if we just have our student file as independent?"

And that leads to one of the most misunderstood ideas in this entire process.

15

"We'll Just File Them as Independent"

At virtually every workshop I hold, I get the same question: "What if we just have them file as independent?"

I understand why this comes up.

First, it's a myth that still floats around online—even though that loophole has been closed for years.

Second, on the surface, it appears to be a very attractive option.

If the forms disregard parent income and assets, the Student Aid Index (SAI) could drop to zero...

Won't this unlock massive financial aid?

Here's the hard truth:
It usually doesn't work as families expect.
And for most, it's not even an option.

Let's break that down.

Not the Silver Bullet It Seems

Even if a student qualifies as independent—either through strict criteria or, in rare cases, professional judgment—the benefit is usually limited.

It may help them qualify for:

- Federal grants
- State grants

But that's not where the largest awards typically come from.

The largest awards usually come from institutional aid—and that's where things get more complicated.

Many schools (especially those using the CSS Profile) may still:

- Request biological parent information
- Require additional documentation

So even if you achieve independent status…

You may not get the outcome you're expecting.

What Defines an Independent Student?

This is where the rules become very clear—and very strict.

An independent student must meet one of the following criteria:

- Age 24 or older
- Enrolled in a graduate or professional program
- Married
- A veteran or active-duty service member
- Has children or dependents (other than a spouse) whom they support
- At any time since age 13: orphaned, in foster care, or a ward of the court

- Legally emancipated or in a court-ordered guardianship
- Determined to be homeless or at risk of homelessness by a qualified authority

That's it.

There's no gray area here.

What Won't Work

This is where the frustration usually sets in.

Because the next questions sound completely reasonable:

"My parents won't help."
"I'm estranged from them."
"They refuse to fill out the forms."
"I support myself."

All valid situations.

None of them qualify.

Another common misunderstanding:

"They file their taxes as independent."

That's tax independence.

That is not FAFSA independence.

The FAFSA rules override tax definitions completely.

"But My Situation is Different..."

Sometimes, it is.

There are rare cases in which a student may qualify for a dependency override through professional judgment.

We'll cover that process later.

But based on experience:

These situations are exceptions.

Not a strategy.

Final Thought

For most families, trying to force independent status isn't a viable path.

And even when it is…

It rarely produces the result they were hoping for.

There are far more effective—and far more realistic—ways to reduce the cost of college.

That's what the rest of this book is about.

What's Next

In this section, we've examined some of the most common assumptions families often hold.

If you've believed any of them, you're not alone.

Most families do at some point.

But as you've seen, these assumptions don't just create confusion—they quietly push families toward more expensive decisions.

Now our focus shifts.

Because the next part of this conversation isn't about forms, formulas, or schools.

It's about something much closer to home.

You.

The parent.

The one holding all of this together.

The one who has worked, saved, planned, and sacrificed to get your student to this moment.

This next section may feel a little different.

But it's one of the most important in the entire book.

Because before we go any further…
We need to make sure you're protected, too.

PART IV

The Trade-offs

"You can't have your cake and eat it too."

We've all heard that phrase.

In everyday life, we see it in small ways.

If you want to lose a few pounds, you probably eat less literal cake.

If you need to get up early, you don't stay up watching The Lincoln Lawyer all night (guilty).

Those are manageable trade-offs.

Temporary ones.

But families often make a trade-off during the college process that is anything but small.

And it doesn't show up right away.

It shows up later.

Quietly.

Over time.

It's the decision to sacrifice your long-term financial security to pay for your student's college education.

Not their future.

Yours.

The retirement you worked decades to build.

The flexibility you were counting on.

The peace of mind you thought you had earned.

And the hardest part?

Most families don't realize they're making this trade-off until it's already in motion.

This may feel like a shift from everything we've discussed so far.

It is.

But it's also the part of this conversation that matters most.

16

Don't Trade Your Retirement for Their Education

At our events, this is the point where the energy shifts.

Up until now, parents have been engaged, asking questions, and taking notes.

Then this topic comes up…

And you can almost feel people doing the math in their heads.

They glance at each other.

And you can tell what they're thinking:

"She's talking about us, isn't she?"

Then, when I meet with those parents a few days later, I hear something like:

"You know, we've been thinking a lot about what you said about retirement…"

Because up until now, we've been talking about the system.

The forms.
The schools.

The strategies.

But now…

We're talking about you.

The parent.

The one who has worked for decades.

Saved.
Sacrificed.
Planned.

And then the questions start:

How much of our retirement should go toward college?
How much longer do I need to work to pay for this?
I'm getting pretty tired of working… do I really need to stay another four years?

In this chapter, I'll share a couple of stories about a teacher and a firefighter. Both thought they needed to work several more years to pay for college.

Teaser alert: they didn't.

The Unsaid Assumption

We are parents.

We sacrifice for our children.

It's what we do, and we are happy to do it.

Sometimes there's even a cultural or personal expectation that we will cover the cost of a prestigious university, no matter the impact on us.

"My child has worked so hard to get here…

I'll sacrifice whatever is necessary to make it happen."

Most of the families we work with are between 45 and 55 years old.

That means something important.

We are much closer to retirement than we were when we started working.

We are also often in our peak earning years, which should ideally be our peak retirement saving years.

But then college shows up.

And here is what I see all the time:

Parents don't run the numbers first.

They make the sacrifices first... and hope the numbers work out later.

It's admirable.

But it's backward.

A Tired Teacher

A few years ago, I met with a teacher and her husband. They had one child, who had the grades to get into several top-ranked, expensive schools.

One of the first things she told us was that she had been a teacher for 30 years and was tired.

So why was she planning to keep working when she had already maxed out her pension and benefits?

To pay for college.

She assumed she needed to work another five years, through her son's high school and college.

After we ran their numbers and reviewed their retirement plan, assets, and college strategy, we scheduled a Zoom meeting to review the results.

One of my favorite moments in this job is when I get to say something like this:

"You don't have to wait five years. You can retire right now."

How was that possible?

Because of many of the principles we've discussed in this book:

We adjusted how their assets were positioned.

We chose schools with strong financial aid potential.

Ironically, her retirement lowered their income, qualifying them for additional aid.

She didn't need to sacrifice more.

She just needed a better plan.

The System Design

There is something important to understand about the college funding system:

Regardless of the strategies you employ, how low your income level, or your assets, the system is designed so that families typically pay something.

Even if your Student Aid Index is very low, there is still typically some level of family responsibility.

In other words, the question is usually not whether you will pay.

The question is how you will pay.

The 3 Ways to Pay for College

When you boil it down, there are really three ways to pay for college:

Pay from income — today's money
Cash flow, budgeting, lifestyle adjustments

Pay from assets — tomorrow's money
Savings, investments, opportunity cost

Borrow — future money
Student loans, parent loans, structured borrowing

Most families I meet:

feel comfortable with the first option but aren't sure how to implement it;
they get nervous about the second, yet often assume it's their only choice;
and don't even want to talk about the third.

A Quick Budget Story

I follow many online college-planning forums and groups, where families share their plans to pay for college using their income.

Some ideas make sense:

"No new cars while the kids are in school." That seems reasonable.

"Eliminating vacations." I am not sure about that… perhaps limit them, but we all need a recharge.

"No more date nights." I see those as vital for marriage preservation, but to each their own.

But I've seen this next one multiple times:

> "I'm going to cut my own hair."

Unless all these people were getting weekly haircuts in Beverly Hills, I'm not sure that's the financial breakthrough we're looking for.

I don't want you to have to cut your own hair.

Let's take that one off the table.

And maybe add back date nights too.

The Borrowing Belief

Most families think:

Borrowing = bad.

What they really mean is…

That borrowing without a plan is bad.

Dr. Stephen Covey's famous principle states:

> **"Begin with the end in mind."**

When you use a GPS, you don't start driving and hope you end up in the right place.

You enter the destination first.

Paying for college should work the same way.

The destination isn't just "pay for college";
It's retirement.

At what age do you want to retire?
How much money do you need to live the life you want?
Where are you today relative to those goals?
What happens if you take a financial detour?

You don't know the best way to pay for college unless you start with the end in mind.

The goal isn't to avoid borrowing, but to use it wisely.

Any of the three ways to pay for college can be financially harmful if it's not aligned with your long-term goals.

Borrowing isn't bad.
Borrowing without a plan is.

A Career Firefighter

We worked with a career firefighter who, like the teacher we discussed earlier, thought he would need to stay on the job until his daughter finished college.

When we first met, he was actually on medical leave after surgery for an injury he sustained while working.

We analyzed his retirement, assets, and daughter's school list, and ultimately used a combination of all three:

Some from income.
Some from assets.
Some from borrowing.

The result?

He was able to retire without ever returning to work after his injury, before his daughter even started college.

It wasn't just relief for him after a long career, but also relief for his family knowing he wouldn't be in harm's way each day.

College shouldn't cost you your happiness.

Or your safety.

A Mom with Rental Properties

Here is another example — and this one surprised me.

I worked with a mom in her late 50s who owned several rental properties. She was the primary breadwinner while her husband dealt with health issues.

They had a modest 529 plan and significant equity in real estate.

I was sure the analysis would say:

Use the 529.

Sell one property.

Pay for college.

But the analysis showed something very different.

The best strategy was to use the 529 and borrow the rest.

The difference between the options amounted to over $1,000,000 more for her in retirement.

An extra million dollars in retirement is no small amount.

This taught me something important:

Even after all these years, I still cannot predict the best answer without running the numbers.

The obvious answer is not always the correct one.

Mistakes That Hurt

There are a few mistakes we see that can cause serious long-term damage.

Taking Money from Retirement Accounts

This is one of the biggest ones.

In certain circumstances, the government may waive the early withdrawal penalty.

But you still pay taxes.

It increases your income.

And then there is opportunity cost.

Let's say you pull out $30,000 per year for four years — $120,000 total.

You didn't just lose $120,000 in your retirement account.

At a 6% return, that decision could cost you roughly **$260,000** fifteen years later.

The most expensive college payments are often those made from retirement accounts—not due to the amount you withdraw, but because of what that money would have grown into.

Borrowing From a 401(k)

Some companies allow you to borrow against your 401(k).

Many parents like this option because they are "paying themselves back."

And technically, that's true.

But the real cost isn't the interest on the loan.

The real cost is that the borrowed money is no longer invested and growing.

So while you are paying yourself back, you may miss out on years of market growth and compounding.

In other words:
The cost isn't the loan.
The cost is what that money would could have become if you had left it alone.

Automatically Ignoring Loans

Compounding is a powerful force.

At 6%, money roughly doubles every 12 years.

If your loan interest rate is similar to long-term investment returns, the decision focuses less on interest and more on protecting retirement and cash flow.

For one family, selling an asset may be the right decision.

For another, borrowing.

For a third, a combination.

There is no universal right answer.

Instead, there is only the right answer for your situation.

The Loan You Won't Qualify For

Dominic says this all the time:

> You can't walk into a bank and take out a retirement loan, saying,
>
> 'Hey, I think I'll live another 30 years—can I borrow $5,000,000?'

It doesn't work that way.

But banks will lend money for education all the time.

Key Takeaway

If there is one thing to remember from this chapter, it is this:

Fund your financial future first.
Finance their education if you must.

There are loans for college, houses, and cars.

There are no loans for retirement.

The goal is not to avoid borrowing.

The goal is to protect your future while you help your child build theirs.

Because a college outcome that costs you your retirement…
Isn't a win.

Fund your financial future first.
Finance their education if you must.

What's Next?

Once you understand the importance of starting with the end in mind, everything changes.

Now we're not just trying to:

"Pay for college."

We're trying to:

Build a plan that works for your entire life.

And what does that take?

Strategy.

PART V

Before the Offer: Building Your Strategy Early

Up to this point, we've spent a lot of time discussing how the system works, the assumptions that cost families money, and the tradeoffs parents need to consider — especially regarding retirement.

Now we shift gears.

In this section, we discuss strategy.

Not after your student is accepted.

Not after the financial aid letters arrive.

Before.

Most factors that determine how much you will pay are shaped long before applications are submitted.

Income.
Assets.
Timing.
School selection.

These are the levers families can actually influence.

Before we go further, I want to make one important note.

I am not a CPA, financial advisor, or attorney. What I'm sharing comes from years of working with families through this process and seeing what works well — and what tends to create problems.

Every family situation is different, and you should absolutely work with qualified professionals when making tax, legal, or investment decisions.

That said, the strategies we're about to discuss have worked well for many families.

They won't apply to every situation. Later, we'll talk about more complex scenarios — business owners, divorce, rental properties, blended families, and other situations that require more nuance.

But for now, we'll focus on core strategies that most families should understand before their student applies to college.

Because the best financial aid strategy is not written in an appeal letter.

It is built years before your student ever applies.

17

Income Strategy – Timing & Controllables

When it comes to financial aid, income plays a major role in determining your Student Aid Index.

But while most people focus on how much they make — and for good reason — that is not the whole story.

Just as important as how much you make is...
When you make it.

It's Not Just How Much – It's When

When you complete the FAFSA, usually around October of your student's senior year, the form uses the "prior-prior" year tax return.

We discussed this earlier, but it's worth revisiting because it's crucial to strategy.

If your student **graduates from high school in 2030** and starts college that fall, the **FAFSA will use your 2028 tax return** to help determine financial aid eligibility.

For most families, that income year falls between:

- The second half of sophomore year
- The first half of junior year

And because you file the FAFSA every year your student is in college, the relevant income years keep shifting forward.

A simple way to think about it:

Tax Year/Student Year	Impacted Financial Aid Year
Sophomore High School	1st Year of College
Junior High School	Sophomore College
Senior High School	Junior College
Freshmen College	Senior College

This is why I keep saying "start earlier than you think." Sophomore-year decisions can affect freshman-year aid.

Of course, school years overlap two calendar years, so this isn't exact, but it's a helpful way to remember the pattern.

So what does that mean?

If you wait until the senior year of high school, the income used for your first-year aid calculation is already largely determined.

This matters because, in our experience, the first year often sets the tone for the remaining years. Schools may use that first year as a baseline, and aid often remains similar unless there is a significant "change in circumstances."

So when you boil this down, the main financial aid planning window often spans from the sophomore year of high school through the student's first year of college.

So if you want to influence the first year of college, you have to start early.

You may be noticing a theme: **The earlier you start, the better.**

What You Can – and Can't – Control

Before we get too far into income strategy, we need to separate two things:

What you can control. And what you can't.

This is not about manipulation or inappropriate actions.

As I tell our clients:

> "I don't look good in orange."

I have no intention of breaking rules and getting myself — or you — into trouble.

This is about understanding the system's rules and making thoughtful decisions within them.

Here are a few things to help you avoid spending time on things you can't control:

Things You May Be Able to Control	Things You Usually Cannot Control
Timing of bonuses or commissions	Base salary, unless self-employed
Timing of stock sales	Required retirement distributions
Capital gains timing	Pension income
Business income timing	RSU vesting schedule
Retirement contributions	Court-ordered payments
HSA contributions	Employer compensation structure
Starting a small business or a side income	Job loss or unexpected income changes
Business deductions	Social Security income

Financial aid planning works best when you focus on the areas you can realistically control.

You don't need to control everything.

But understanding what you can control matters, especially when it comes to timing.

The same income in a different year can produce a very different financial aid outcome.

Employed vs. Self-Employed

There is a significant difference between W-2 employees and business owners in financial aid planning.

For this discussion, let's define them this way:

W-2 employee: Someone who works for a company they do not own and receives a W-2 at the end of the year.

Self-employed or business owner: Someone who owns or co-owns a business. This person may still receive a W-2 from the business, depending on its structure, but they are still an owner.

W-2 employees generally have less control over earnings and deductions, which means less control over Adjusted Gross Income.

Business owners often have more flexibility regarding distributions, deductions, retirement contributions, and business expenses—all of which can affect AGI.

That does not mean W-2 employees should throw up their hands and say:

"I knew it. We won't qualify."

There are still effective strategies you can employ.

AGI & The W-2 Employee

Earlier, we talked about above-the-line and below-the-line deductions.

The "line" is your Adjusted Gross Income.

For W-2 employees, many common deductions—mortgage interest, certain credits, and other tax benefits—fall below the line.

They may reduce your tax bill.

But they do not reduce your AGI.

The above-the-line options are usually more limited.

The most common include:

- 401(k) contributions
- Other retirement plan contributions
- Health Savings Account (HSA) contributions

These can lower AGI, potentially improving financial aid positioning.

For some families, increasing retirement or HSA contributions during the planning years may reduce AGI enough to make a meaningful difference.

Of course, you have to watch cash flow.

Some families hesitate to contribute more to retirement during the college years because they are worried about paying the college bill.

But in some cases, those additional contributions may lower AGI enough to improve aid eligibility.

And that ties back to something we discussed earlier:

You can borrow money to pay for college.
You cannot borrow money for retirement.

What You Can Control (Timing Examples)

As a W-2 employee, you may have control over certain timing decisions.

For example:

- Timing of bonuses or commissions
- Timing of stock sales
- Timing of capital gains
- Retirement contributions
- HSA contributions
- Starting a side business

Are you due for a large bonus or commission?

In some cases, you may be able to ask your employer to defer it until the following year.

That may require approval, and it may not always be possible.

But if it means a $50,000 swing in income during a key financial aid year, it may be worth asking.

Are you thinking about selling vested stock?

It may be better to sell in a year that isn't a key financial aid income year.

These decisions require planning and communication.
Please do not leave them until the last minute.

Example: Severance Payout & Hiring Bonus Timing

Several years ago, we worked with a high-level executive who was downsized from her position and received a generous severance package.

She was highly marketable, so it wasn't long before she received an offer from another company.

Because she was in demand, the new company also offered a signing bonus.

She could not change the timing of the severance payout, but as we reviewed her financial situation, we realized the signing bonus could create a problem.

It was reasonable to expect a financial aid office to overlook a one-time severance package.

Asking them to overlook both a severance package and a large signing bonus in the same year?

Much harder.

So she asked the new company if she could defer the signing bonus until the following year.

After a short approval process, they agreed.

By splitting the severance and signing bonus into different years, we were able to present each as a separate one-time income event.

That made it much easier for the financial aid office to evaluate the situation accurately.

Timing and planning matter more than most families realize.

AGI & The Business Owner

When prospective clients tell us they own a business, I have to admit…

We get a little excited.

We work successfully with many W-2 families, but business owners often have more options to manage AGI.

Business owners may have the ability to:

- Deduct legitimate business expenses
- Control distributions
- Adjust retirement contributions
- Purchase equipment
- Manage retained earnings
- Use certain tax strategies

All of these can affect what ultimately appears as Adjusted Gross Income.

In the next chapter, I'll show you some incredibly effective strategies we've seen for business owners.

Yes, they may require documentation and extra work.

But the rewards can be significant.

And you can probably guess what I'll say next.

You have to start early.

What If I Don't Have a Business

This is worth considering because many families are already sitting on something valuable.

A skill.
A hobby.
An area of expertise.
A passion project.

They just haven't formalized it.

Over the years, we've worked with families who:

- Turned a hobby into a small business
- Began consulting in their area of expertise
- Started an Etsy or e-commerce store
- Wrote and sold a book
- Monetized woodworking, photography, coaching, or tutoring
- Formalized existing freelance work.

In many cases, these weren't dramatic life changes.

They were structured versions of something already happening.

We are not suggesting that anyone start a business solely for tax purposes. The IRS requires legitimate business intent and a real profit motive.

But if you've been on the fence about launching something aligned with your skills or interests, doing so early — and operating it properly — may create opportunities to structure income thoughtfully before the financial aid years begin.

And building something real, even something small, can create more options than most families realize.

Example: Executives & Woodworking

A few years ago, I met with a family in Northern California.

Both parents had solid jobs, and their combined Adjusted Gross Income was in the mid-$200,000 range.

They were worried their son, who was a sophomore at the time, would not qualify for any financial aid.

As I got to know them, I discovered that the father had a woodworking hobby.

When I asked if he used space at the house for it, his wife laughed and said,

"It's the entire garage and then some."

He made furniture for fun and occasionally built pieces for friends, charging them for materials and a little extra for his time.

That was a business opportunity.

That's what I mean when I say many families are already sitting on something that could become a small business.

Once they formalized their woodworking as a legitimate business, their CPA was able to deduct legitimate business expenses such as tools, materials, and a portion of the garage workspace.

Those deductions lowered their AGI enough for their daughter to qualify for the Cal Grant and receive free tuition at a California state school.

The proper use of legitimate business deductions can make a meaningful difference.

Timing Matters

Up to this point, we've focused on timing income and understanding what you can and cannot control.

But for business owners — or families considering starting a business — there are a few additional strategies that can significantly impact how income appears on your tax return.

In the next chapter, we'll walk through some of the most common strategies we see during the financial aid year.

18

Income Strategy – Advanced Strategies for Business Owners

Business owners often have more flexibility than W-2 employees in how income flows through their tax return.

That does not mean they can fabricate numbers.

It does mean that when a business is properly structured, there may be legitimate ways to reduce Adjusted Gross Income for financial aid purposes without reducing the family's actual cash flow.

In this chapter, I'm going to walk through three strategies we've seen work well for business owners:

- The Augusta Rule
- Accountable plans
- Family payroll

If you don't currently own a business, I still encourage you to read this chapter. If the last chapter didn't nudge you in that direction, this one might.

Before we go further, an important reminder:

This chapter is not about doing anything aggressive or inappropriate.

It is about understanding the rules and using them correctly.

If you read this chapter and realize one of these strategies may apply to your family, we have more detailed tools and templates available on our website, including sample documents, checklists, and implementation guides.

Why These Strategies Matter

Adjusted Gross Income heavily influences financial aid formulas.

Many families assume the only way to lower AGI is to make less money.

That is not true.

For business owners, the opportunity is often not about earning less.

It is about properly structuring income, reimbursements, and deductions so the tax return accurately reflects the business.

When done correctly, these strategies may:

- Lower Adjusted Gross Income
- Shift income to another taxpayer
- Convert personal income into legitimate business reimbursements
- Move money from the business to the family without increasing personal taxable income

During the financial aid years, this can make a meaningful difference.

Strategy #1: The Augusta Rule

The Augusta Rule allows business owners to rent their personal residence to their business for meetings or events for up to 14 days per year.

The business can deduct the rental expense, and the homeowner does not report the rental income on their personal tax return, as long as the rules are followed.

In plain English:

Money moves from the business to the family, but personal taxable income does not increase.

This can be powerful during the financial aid years.

Example

Let's say a business owner rents their home to the business for 10 meeting days during the year at $1,000 per day.

That results in $10,000 in rental payments.

- The business deducts $10,000.
- The homeowner receives $10,000 tax-free.
- Personal taxable income does not increase.

The family still has the money.

But their AGI may be lower than it would otherwise be.

This is the kind of difference that can matter in financial aid calculations.

Strategy #2: Accountable Plan

An accountable plan allows a business to reimburse the owner or employee for legitimate business expenses without treating those reimbursements as taxable income.

Common reimbursable expenses may include:

- Mileage
- Home office expenses
- Internet
- Software
- Supplies
- Other legitimate business costs

The business deducts the expense.

The reimbursement does not appear as taxable income on the personal return, as long as the rules are followed and documentation is maintained.

Without an accountable plan, many business owners simply take more income from the business to cover these costs.

That increases taxable income.

With an accountable plan, the business reimburses the expenses directly.

Same money.
Different tax treatment.

And during the financial aid years, that difference can matter.

Example

Let's say a business owner has:

- $5,000 of business mileage
- $3,000 of home office expenses
- $2,000 of internet, software, and supplies

Without an accountable plan, the owner may take an extra $10,000 in income to cover those costs.

With an accountable plan, the business properly reimburses those expenses.

Result:

- The business deducts the expenses.
- The business owner receives reimbursement.
- Personal taxable income does not increase by $10,000.

Strategy #3: Family Payroll

Family payroll involves a business owner hiring their children to do legitimate work in the family business and paying them a reasonable wage.

The business deducts the wages as a business expense.

The child may pay little or no federal income tax, depending on how much they earn and their standard deduction.

This strategy can shift income from the parent's higher tax bracket to the child's lower tax bracket while reducing the parent's reported income.

This strategy isn't limited to children of college age.

Younger children can also be paid for legitimate, age-appropriate work.

We've seen families pay high school students, middle school students, and even younger children for actual business tasks, such as:

- Organizing materials
- Helping at events
- Data entry
- Cleaning equipment
- Packaging products
- Filing or scanning documents

The key is simple:

The work must be real.
The pay must be reasonable.
The documentation must be maintained.

Why This Matters for Financial Aid

If a business owner earns an additional $15,000, that may increase the parent's AGI.

If the business instead pays $15,000 to children for legitimate work:

- The business deducts the wages.
- The child may pay little or no federal income tax.
- The parents' taxable income may be lower.
- The family still keeps the money.

From the family's perspective, the money didn't leave the household;
It was simply reported differently.

During the financial aid years, that can matter.

Example

For instance, if a business pays one child $15,000 for legitimate work performed during the year:

- The business deducts $15,000.
- The child may owe little or no federal income tax.
- The parents' taxable income may be lower.
- The family still keeps the $15,000.

The money stays in the household — it was simply reported differently.

Real-Life Examples

In our own business, our children have contributed in various ways over the years.

When our son was younger, he helped set up clients in our systems, organize files, and assist with simple administrative tasks.

When our daughter was in college, she helped at events by greeting families, directing people, managing sign-in sheets, and assisting with setup and breakdown.

These were legitimate tasks we would otherwise have paid someone else to do.

That is the key question:

Would you have to pay someone else to do this work if your child did not do it?

If the answer is yes, it may be legitimate payroll work.

Examples of Jobs Children Can Do (By Age)

One of the most frequent questions parents ask me is, "What could we actually pay them to do?"

Here are some common examples.

Younger Children

- Cleaning office space
- Organizing supplies
- Shredding documents
- Labeling envelopes or folders
- Packaging products
- Filing paperwork
- Basic cleaning tasks
- Simple inventory counting

Middle School / Early High School

- Data entry
- Scanning documents
- Organizing digital files
- Social media posting
- Preparing mailers
- Assembling packets
- Event setup and breakdown
- Photography for the business
- Basic website updates
- Customer follow-up emails (template-based)

High School / College Students

- Social media management
- Website updates
- Graphic design
- Video editing
- Customer service
- Event staffing
- Scheduling
- Bookkeeping assistance
- Marketing assistance
- CRM/data management
- Research projects
- Writing blog posts or newsletters

Many families are surprised by how many legitimate tasks exist once they start looking.

Important Reminders for a Family Payroll

There are a few rules you need to follow:

- The work must be legitimate

- The pay must be reasonable
- Hours should be tracked
- Job descriptions should be written
- Payroll should be processed properly
- W-2s should be issued
- Documentation should be maintained
- Your CPA should be involved

We strongly recommend using a professional payroll company such as Gusto, ADP, or Paychex. Most families prefer not to handle payroll tax filings themselves.

Again, the goal is not to be aggressive.

The goal is to properly structure legitimate work and document it well.

Tax Strategy Summary

Before we move on, let's summarize these three strategies.

Strategy	What It Is	Why It Helps
Augusta Rule	Rent your home to your business for meetings or events for up to 14 days per year	Moves money from the business to the family without increasing personal taxable income, if done correctly
Accountable Plan	Reimburse yourself for legitimate business expenses	Allows the business to deduct expenses without treating reimbursements as personal income
Family Payroll	Pay children for legitimate work in the business	Shifts income from the parent to the child and may reduce the parent's AGI

These strategies can be powerful tools for business owners—but documentation and proper implementation are essential.

Each strategy is designed to do one or more of the following:

- Reduce business income
- Reduce Adjusted Gross Income
- Shift income to another taxpayer
- Move money from the business to the family without increasing personal taxable income.

These are not magic tricks.

They are planning tools.

And like all planning tools, they only work when used correctly.

Final Thoughts on Business Strategies

These strategies are not shortcuts.

They require:

- Proper documentation
- Good record keeping
- Coordination with your CPA
- Planning ahead

But when done correctly, they can significantly change how income appears on your tax return during the financial aid years.

And as we've discussed throughout this section:

Financial aid planning is often not about making less money.
It is about making smart decisions about when and how income appears.

For business owners, this can create opportunities that many families don't even realize exist.

19

The Impact of Assets

When I talk to a new family, they usually start their with income.

Then they might mention retirement accounts or 529 plans.

But it often takes a little digging to uncover the brokerage account, the rental property, or the paid-off house inherited from Grandma.

That is not because families are trying to hide anything.

Most of the time, they simply don't realize those assets matter.

I once met with a very nice woman from the Midwest who was incredibly well prepared for our call. She had spreadsheets, tax returns, and neatly organized notes.

On one of her spreadsheets, I saw a mention of rental income, so I asked about the properties.

She explained how she had included the rental income.

But my question wasn't really about the income. It was about the properties themselves.

She looked a little confused and said something like, "Well, those are more like my retirement account."

She is a joy to work with and incredibly smart. But like many families, she assumed the school would treat those properties differently because they were part of her long-term retirement plan.

They aren't.

This is common.

Families are so focused on income as the driving force behind their Student Aid Index that they often underestimate how much their assets affect the index.

The financial aid system doesn't just ask how much you have.
It asks where that money sits.

And that distinction matters.

In the coming chapters, we will discuss strategies that may help mitigate the impact of what you're about to learn.

Why Assets Matter More Than You Might Think

Counselors, articles, and online advice all tend to focus on income first. Families then read that assets are assessed at such low percentages that they assume they don't matter much.

But there are really two things happening at the same time:

- How federal and state programs treat assets
- How institutions treat assets

And those two worlds are not always the same.

FAFSA vs. CSS - Two Different Worlds

While all humans are created equal, assets are not.

Some assets are treated favorably. Some are ignored. Some are counted more heavily than families expect.

For example:

- The equity in your primary residence does not count on the FAFSA.
- Many CSS schools do count that equity.
- Retirement accounts do not count on the FAFSA.
- CSS schools often consider them as part of your broader financial picture.
- Brokerage and savings accounts are counted in both systems, but often at different rates and with different practical consequences.

The easiest way to explain the difference is this:

The FAFSA asks:

"What does the federal formula say you can afford?"

The CSS Profile asks:

"Looking at your broader financial life, *what do we think* you can afford?"

That distinction matters.

A family may seem eligible for aid under the FAFSA formula but receive a very different answer from a CSS school.

That does not mean anyone made a mistake. It means the school is using a different lens.

The FAFSA gets most of the attention. But the schools — especially those that use the CSS Profile — play a major role in determining your ability to pay.

FAFSA = *What does the formula say you can afford?*
CSS Profile = *What does the school think you can afford?*

An Example of the Math

Let's use a simplified family example:

- $200,000 in savings
- $400,000 in rental equity
- $600,000 in primary residence equity
- Total net worth in these assets: $1.2 million

FAFSA Formula Might Count

- $200,000 in savings
- $400,000 in rental equity

The FAFSA formulas vary year to year, but a rough average parent asset assessment is about **5.64%**.

So:
$600,000 × 5.64% = about $34,000 added to the SAI

Notice that this does not include income. This is just the asset side.

These percentages vary by school, so treat this as a simplified example rather than a universal rule.

CSS Profile Schools May Count

- $200,000 in savings
- $400,000 in rental equity
- $600,000 in primary residence equity

Again, school formulas vary, but let's use a rough range of 8–10%.

$1,200,000 × 8–10% = $96,000–$120,000 institutional contribution

Now let's plug those into the need formula:

Cost of Attendance – Student Aid Index = Need

FAFSA school:
$90,000 – $34,000 = $56,000 of need

CSS school:
$90,000 – ($96,000 to $120,000) = negative need, which in plain English means:
"We think you can afford this."

That's a very different outcome.

All Hope is Not Lost

Please don't read that example and think, "Well, we're doomed."

You're not.

This is where school selection, timing, and asset positioning become important.

The purpose of this chapter is not to scare you.

This chapter shows you what the system sees. In the next chapter, we'll discuss how to use that information.

Assets Reset Every Year

Income can change dramatically from year to year.

Assets are no different.

They are reported annually.

So if a family has $500,000 in non-retirement assets and a school effectively assesses 5% each year, that could mean:

$25,000 per year × 4 years = $100,000 of impact

Assets are not a one-time issue.

They can affect all four years.

Asset Categories Explained

As you may have already guessed, this is not a perfectly straightforward conversation.

I'm going to give you the general rules and the most common patterns we see.

Please remember: this does not yet include school selection strategy or the asset-positioning strategies we'll cover next.

I need to show you the "how" before we get into what to do with it.

To get us started, here is a straightforward chart that breaks down the most common asset types we see.

Asset Type	FAFSA	CSS Schools (Typical)
Parent assets (Averaged)	~ 5.64%	~8–12%
Student assets	20%	20–25%
Cash	~5%	~8–12%
Brokerage	~5%	~8–12%
529 Plans	Counted	Counted
Primary home equity	Ignored	~3–8%
Rental properties	~5%	~8–12%
Business value	Ignored (<100 employees)	Often considered
Retirement	Not counted	Considered indirectly
Non-custodial parent	Ignored	Often counted (~8–12%)
Cash-value life insurance	Ignored	Often ignored

This is why two schools can look at the exact same family and produce very different aid offers.

I'll break these down in more detail below.

And yes, if you're someone who likes to skip ahead, feel free. My husband always does. I've learned not to fight it.

But I'd encourage you to at least read the sections that apply most to you before jumping ahead to the strategy chapter. It will help those strategies make a lot more sense.

If you do skip ahead and get stuck, just meander back here.

I won't say, "I told you so."

Parent vs. Student Assets

One thing that may have jumped out at you immediately from the chart is that student assets are counted much more heavily than parent assets.

Money in a child's name is weighted roughly four times more heavily than money in a parent's name when it comes to financial aid.

That makes sense from the school's perspective.

Students are assumed to have very few obligations, while parents are assumed to have many.

This applies across most asset categories.

If Grandma has been quietly saving money in an account where the child is the sole account holder, we appreciate her generosity, but this can still hurt.

Over the years, we have seen many generous grandparents save money for college since their grandchild was very young.

Parents often have a rude awakening when they realize how significantly student-owned money can reduce their eligibility for aid.

The good news?

That can often be fixed or planned around.

In practice, student accounts are also more often set up with a joint account holder, which can help.

Families with significant assets sometimes put money in a child's name for tax reasons.

That can be smart in one context and painful in another, like college.

This is one of those times when your view of money during the college years often differs greatly from how you view it at any other time.

UTMA/UGMA Accounts

These don't need a full chapter, but they do deserve mention.

UTMA and UGMA accounts are custodial investment accounts for children. The money legally belongs to the child, but an adult manages it until the child reaches the age of majority, typically 18 or 21, depending on the state.

For financial aid purposes, these accounts are **treated as student assets**, even before the child has legal control.

Many families do not even realize these accounts exist, especially if grandparents opened them.

That can create a surprising reduction in aid eligibility.

The good news is that those assets can often be spent on the child's behalf before the vesting age.

Depending on the timing and situation, that can be helpful.

It is also worth remembering that once the child reaches the vesting age, the money is entirely theirs to use as they wish, which may not be for college.

Cash & Brokerage Accounts

These are among the first assets the government and colleges consider, as they view them as a primary source of repayment.

I get questions like:
"What if it's in a long-term CD?"
"What if it's in bonds?"
"What if the account is down in value?"

Same answer: **It doesn't matter much to them.**

The reasoning is that these are liquid or investable assets, and the formulas already account for some of this by not assessing them on a dollar-for-dollar basis.

The FAFSA includes over 5% of the parent assets.

CSS schools often use a higher effective rate—sometimes materially higher.

No matter how you slice it, colleges pay close attention to cash and brokerage accounts.

What if They Are in a Living Trust?

This is one of the most common misunderstandings about trusts.

A living trust is an estate planning tool. It helps determine how assets are managed and transferred and can help avoid probate.

But you are still the beneficial owner of those assets.

That means the FAFSA and CSS Profile generally still treat those assets as yours.

A living trust is revocable, meaning you can change it.

That is very different from some irrevocable trust situations.

I recently worked with a student whose father had passed away. When he died, a portion of the trust became irrevocable. The mother could receive income from it, which was reflected in her AGI, but she could not sell, transfer, reinvest, or otherwise control the asset.

The son was the beneficiary, but he could not access it until his mother passed away.

In that case, I was able to get the school to overlook the asset.

But in general, and contrary to what parents often hear, **assets in a living trust and many other trusts must still be reported.**

Assets are not all treated equally.

Some have modest effects.

Others can dramatically change the outcome.

Next, we'll look at two areas that surprise families more than almost anything else:

Real estate and college savings plans.

20

Real Estate & Financial Aid

If income is the topic families discuss the most, real estate is often the surprising element they discover later.

Families in high-cost housing markets feel this most acutely because equity can grow substantially even when cash flow has not.

Primary Home Equity

This is one of the clearest places where the difference between FAFSA and CSS schools becomes apparent.

On the FAFSA, your primary residence does not count.

You do not list it.

And yes, I still see families accidentally include it. Don't be one of them.

On the CSS Profile, you will usually have to disclose both the value of your home and the amount of equity you have in it.

Whether and how a school counts that equity varies significantly.

Some schools use what is often referred to as a **home equity special assessment.**

In general, schools may handle home equity in one of three ways:

Equity-to-Asset Model
They treat home equity like another parent asset and apply a percentage to it.

Income Cap Model
They cap the amount of home equity they will consider based on a multiple of your income.

Income Stream Model
They assume you could borrow against your home and use that borrowing capacity as part of your payment ability.

Confused yet?

That's normal.

Here is a simplified example.

Home Equity Math Example

- AGI = $250,000
- Home value = $1.5 million
- Mortgage = $500,000
- Equity = $1,000,000

Equity-to-Asset Model:
5–8% × $1,000,000 = $50,000–$80,000

Income Cap Model:
Cap equity at 1.5–2× income = $250,000–$375,000
Apply 5–8% = $12,500–$30,000

Income Stream Model:

The school assumes you can borrow $200,000
They assume some of that borrowing capacity will support college payments.
The impact could easily be $18,000 or potentially higher, depending on how they view your broader financial picture.
This is why many families — especially in California and other high-cost areas — feel like they are being assessed for much more than the simple 5% they read about online.

School Examples

Policies change, but here are some common examples:

Often ignore home equity:
Stanford, Princeton, UPenn, University of Chicago, MIT

Often use equity-to-asset models:
USC, Tulane, NYU, Boston College, Boston University, University of Richmond

Often use income-cap models:
Harvard, Yale, Columbia, Duke, Northwestern, Rice

Often use income-stream models:
University of Miami, Emory, Northeastern

Rental Properties

Rental properties can affect aid in three ways:

- The income affects AGI
- The equity counts as an asset
- CSS schools may add back depreciation and certain deductions

The **FAFSA uses** the tax return.
CSS schools often **analyze** your tax return.

From a school's perspective, rental property may be viewed as something that can be sold, borrowed against, or used to help pay for college.

Whether that feels realistic to you is not always the point.

That is often how the school perceives it.

Income

Rental income usually flows through Schedule E and becomes part of AGI.

If the property generates positive income, that may increase AGI.

If it incurs a loss, that may decrease AGI.

However, CSS schools often add back items like depreciation and certain losses when evaluating your actual cash flow.

So a property that appears to benefit you on a tax return may still negatively impact you in the institutional formula.

Equity

Rental equity generally counts for both FAFSA and CSS calculations.

For FAFSA purposes, rental equity is treated as a parental asset and is typically assessed at the parent rate.

For CSS schools, rental property is often viewed as fully available and assessed at a higher effective rate.

Rental Property Math Example

Scenario:

- Salary: $150,000
- Rental Value: $900,000
- Mortgage: $400,000

- Rental Property Equity: $500,000
- Gross Rent: $48,000/year
- Rental Mortgage Interest: $12,000
- Rental Depreciation: $25,000
- Rental Expenses: $10,000

FAFSA *income* view
$48,000 – $12,000 – $25,000 – $10,000 = about **$1,000 of rental income**
AGI = about **$151,000**

CSS *income* view
Depreciation and some expenses may be added back.
The same property could be viewed as producing $**36,000 or more of usable income.**
AGI equivalent = **$186,000 or more**

FAFSA *asset* view
$500,000 × about 5% = roughly **$25,000 added to SAI**

CSS *asset* view
$500,000 × 8–12% = roughly **$40,000–$60,000 institutional contribution**

Those are very different outcomes.

And this is why rental properties are among the biggest surprises for the families I meet.

The challenge is that schools often view rental properties as nearly equivalent to cash.

The good news?

There are strategies to address that, and we'll get into them next.

Rental Property Summary

Rental properties can affect aid in three ways:

- The equity counts as an asset
- The income affects AGI
- CSS schools may add back depreciation and deductions

The FAFSA **uses** your tax return.

CSS schools often **analyze** your tax return.

Regardless of the application type (FAFSA or CSS Profile), schools consider rental properties to be assets that can be sold or used as collateral to pay tuition.

Whether that is realistic or not is not their concern.

21

College Savings, Business Assets & Special Situations

By now, you've seen that not all assets are treated the same.

Some are obvious:

- Cash.
- Brokerage accounts.

Families usually know that they have an impact on financial aid.

Real estate can cause some confusion.

The next group of assets can be even trickier.

These are the assets and situations that often create the most confusion because they sit in the gray area between:

"Everyone told me this was a good idea."

and

"What?… this affects financial aid too?"

- 529 plans.
- Business ownership.

- Retirement accounts.
- Non-custodial parents.
- Insurance-based assets.

None of these is inherently good or bad.

Many of them exist because families made thoughtful decisions years earlier.

The challenge is that college planning sometimes views those decisions through a very different lens.

I've had parents say things like:

"We saved for college because everyone told us to."
"We built the business to support our family."
"We increased retirement contributions because that seemed responsible."

Those decisions may still be absolutely right.

But once college enters the picture, it helps to understand how the system views them.

Because this is where many families discover that financial aid is not only about how much money exists.

It is also about:

Where it sits
Who owns it
And the story that asset tells about your ability to pay, which doesn't always match your reality.

Let's start with one of the most misunderstood areas in all of college planning:

529 plans.

529 College Savings Plans

We talked about 529 plans earlier, and I want to revisit them because they are among the most misunderstood aspects of college planning.

I remain generally cautious about 529 plans when financial aid is a major concern.

Not because they are bad — they are not.

But because families are often told they are the best way to save for college, without anyone explaining how they may affect financial aid later.

Technically, 529 plans are usually treated as a parent asset and are typically counted at roughly 5% in federal formulas.

However, in practice — especially at private schools using their own institutional formulas — large 529 balances can influence how schools assess your ability to pay.

Because the money is already earmarked for college, FAFSA and CSS schools may expect those funds to be used before institutional aid is awarded.

So while the percentage in the formula may look modest on paper, the real-world impact can be much larger than families expect.

The Multi-Child Surprise

Another point that catches families off guard is this:

If the parent owns the 529, it is generally treated as a parent asset regardless of whether the beneficiary is the oldest child, a younger sibling, or if it is changed later.

Sometimes, families believe they have a simple solution for a 529 balance that is getting too high.

They say to me, "Well then, I'll just switch the beneficiary to the younger child."

I understand the instinct.

Unfortunately, that usually does not resolve the problem.

Why?

Because, for **financial aid purposes, the key issue is who owns the account,** not which child is named as the beneficiary.

Changing the beneficiary does not remove the asset from the financial aid picture.

And here is the bigger surprise for many families:

If you have multiple 529 accounts for multiple children, schools often look at the **total parent-owned 529 balance,** not just the account earmarked for the student currently applying to college.

So if a family has:

- $30,000 for Child A
- $30,000 for Child B
- $30,000 for Child C

The school will likely view that as **$90,000 in parent assets,** even if only one child is heading to college right now.

The school is not asking,

"Which child is this account for?"

They are asking,

"How much money have the parents already set aside for college?"

This is one more reason why 529 planning can be more nuanced than families realize — especially when there are multiple children in the family.

529s In Plain English

The more money you've already set aside specifically for college, the less help some schools may determine you need.

That can be a challenging conversation.

I've had parents say to me,

"So I did everything right, and now I feel like I'm being penalized."

I understand why it feels that way.

And that is exactly why I am so passionate about explaining this now, before it's too late to plan.

That said, context matters.

If a family has less than about $30,000 in a 529, we usually don't worry too much about it. At that level, the impact is often modest, and the tax advantages and simplicity may outweigh any planning downside.

The juice often isn't worth the squeeze.

But once balances reach the six figures — $100,000, $200,000, or more — planning becomes much more important.

529 plans absolutely do have real advantages:

- Tax-free growth
- Tax-free withdrawals for education
- Possible state tax deductions
- Flexibility to change beneficiaries

Just be aware that in practice, large 529 balances can have a meaningful impact on financial aid.

A 529 plan is often a great way to save for college.
It is not always advantageous for qualifying for financial aid.

Both things can be true.

Business Value

Here again, we see a major difference between FAFSA and CSS schools.

And just to be clear, this section is about **business value as an asset,** not business income. We covered income in the prior chapters.

FAFSA

If the business has fewer than 100 employees, business assets are generally not counted on the FAFSA.

That's a big advantage.

If the business has more than 100 employees, I strongly suggest getting professional help due to the significant complexity and potential for error.

CSS Profile

CSS schools may ask about:

- Equipment
- Cash on hand
- Retained earnings
- Business real estate
- General business value

This varies significantly by school.

But in general, FAFSA often ignores business assets for businesses with fewer than 100 employees, while CSS schools may request and consider them regardless of size.

Retirement Accounts

This part confuses many people, so let's simplify it.

The Retirement Misconception
"Retirement accounts don't count."

That statement is true.
And incomplete.

On the FAFSA, you do not report retirement accounts.

On the CSS Profile, you usually do.

Does that mean CSS schools expect you to drain your retirement to pay for college?

No.

But many of them will view retirement balances as part of your larger financial picture.

That can show up in three main ways.

Ability to Borrow
Schools may assume:

- You could take a 401(k) loan
- You could reduce retirement contributions
- You have long-term financial strength

So, retirement can influence contribution expectations even if its value isn't directly assessed, as with cash.

Retirement Contributions Added Back as Income
This is a significant factor.
If parents contribute:

- $20,000 to a 401(k)

- $10,000 to a SEP IRA
- $15,000 to a Solo 401(k)

CSS schools often consider those contributions as available income.

So the strategy of reducing AGI through retirement contributions:

- Often helps with FAFSA
- May not help at CSS schools

Asset Strength Adjustment
Some schools evaluate your overall financial situation — including retirement, age, years until retirement, number of children in school, and other assets — and manually adjust the expected contribution.

In simple terms:

The retirement asset may not be assessed directly, unlike cash or brokerage accounts.

However, it can still influence how a school views your overall ability to pay.

Non-Custodial Parent Assets

We will delve into this when we discuss complicated family situations.

But it is worth noting here that while the FAFSA ignores the non-custodial parent, CSS schools often do not.

Even if that parent is minimally involved.
Even if they live abroad.
Even if you are absolutely certain they are crazy.

And one more wrinkle:
If you are the custodial parent and are remarried, the assets of your new spouse may also be considered.

This can create significant and unexpected outcomes.

Insurance-Based Cash Value Assets

Certain insurance-based financial products may be treated differently than traditional savings or brokerage accounts in financial aid calculations.

In general, the cash value of **properly structured** life insurance policies is not reported as a parent asset on the FAFSA. Many schools also do not assess these values directly in their institutional formulas, though treatment can vary across institutions and policy structures.

As a result, some families are surprised to learn that two households with similar net worth may appear very different for financial aid purposes depending on how their assets are held.

That said, insurance-based products are not inherently "better" savings vehicles. They come with costs, complexity, and trade-offs that must be evaluated carefully.

I mention them here simply because understanding how different asset types are treated is important for a complete financial aid picture.

Asset Summary

We covered a lot across these chapters.

If you came into this section thinking assets were just a minor conversation compared to income, you may be viewing them differently now.

That is normal.

Assets can affect financial aid in ways many families never anticipate.

We looked at:

Cash and brokerage accounts
Student-owned assets
Real estate
529 plans
Business ownership
Retirement accounts
Special family situations

And perhaps most importantly, we examined how FAFSA and CSS schools often view those assets very differently.

If some of this felt a bit overwhelming, take a breath.

You do not need to resolve everything right now.

The purpose of these chapters was not to alarm you.

It was to help you understand what the system perceives.

Because once you understand that…

You can begin making better decisions about:

Timing
Positioning
School selection
And strategy

That is where we are headed next.

We've spent time understanding the rules.

Now let's discuss what to do with them.

22

Asset Strategy – Timing & Positioning

The last three chapters were not just a pile of information.

They were a collection of conversations I have with families every year.

Cash-poor and property-rich families.
Real estate investors with strong assets but tight monthly cash flow.
Families with modest incomes and surprisingly large accounts.
Families who saved diligently and are now wondering if their savings will hurt them.

After discussing how assets are viewed, many parents have the same reaction:

"Wow. This is worse than I thought."

And that's when I usually say:
"Hang in there. This is where the strategy begins."

This chapter is about avoiding panic and positioning for success.

The Four Gauges of the Financial Aid System

Earlier in the book, I used the analogy of car dashboard gauges.

For financial aid, four gauges matter most:

Income.
Assets.
Timing.
School selection.

We've already discussed income and how timing affects it.

Now we're going to focus on assets—specifically, how ownership, timing, and positioning can dramatically change the school's perception of them.

General Timing

Income is historical.
Assets are a snapshot.

Income is usually based on the prior-prior-year tax return.

Assets are reported as of the day you submit the FAFSA or CSS Profile.

That difference matters.

Because while you cannot change a tax year that has already closed, you may still have options for your assets before filing the forms.

Financial aid is not just about what you have.

It is about what you have when you file — and how it is positioned when you report it.

Income is historical
Assets are a snapshot

Start With Ownership

Asset ownership is often overlooked, yet it is one of the simplest and most effective ways to reduce potential issues.

How an asset is held can significantly impact your financial aid situation.

Put another way:

The same $50,000 can hurt you a lot, a little, or not at all, depending on who owns it.

Parent vs. Student Assets - Start Here

If you read the last chapter, you already saw how much more damaging student-held assets can be than parent-held assets.

As a rule, assets in a student's name carry about four times the weight of assets in a parent's name.

If the FAFSA assesses a parent's assets at around 5%, a student's assets may be assessed at 20%.

The same general idea applies to CSS schools as well, where parent assets are often treated more favorably than student assets.

The logic is fairly straightforward.

Parents have households to run, emergencies to plan for, and real-life obligations.

Students typically do not.

Schools assume a larger portion of a student's money is available for college, which is one reason why ownership matters so much.

Accounts and Assets in Student Name

If possible, moving assets out of a student's name can be one of the fastest ways to reduce the damage they cause.

Often, transferring the asset to a parent is enough.

Sometimes, depending on the overall financial picture, it may make sense for another trusted person — such as a grandparent — to own the asset instead.

A few years ago, I worked with a single mom who was right on the bubble for Cal Grant eligibility, which has strict asset ceilings.

There were a few accounts in the daughter's name that were assessed at the higher student-asset rate and also pushed Mom over the limit.

Grandma was a lovely woman doing everything she could to help, so transferring those assets into her name was a quick solution.

And remember — these changes do not necessarily have to be permanent.

Assets are reviewed as a snapshot in time.

That said, keep in mind that you will file the FAFSA every year, and many schools — especially highly selective private institutions — may require the CSS Profile annually as well.

UTMA/UGMA Accounts

These are tricky because, as we discussed earlier, they are considered student assets regardless of who originally set them up.

Importantly, they are treated as student assets even if the child has not yet reached the age of control.

In my experience, these accounts are often opened by grandparents.

This can create an additional challenge because parents sometimes don't even know the account exists.

If you do not know an account exists, it is hard to report it accurately.

And if it's only discovered after college, that means the school likely never had a chance to account for it in the aid calculation.

UTMA to 529 Conversion

I will mention this strategy, with the full disclosure that I haven't yet found a situation where it was my preferred solution.

It is possible to convert a UTMA into a UTMA 529.

This is not the same as a standard parent-owned 529. In a UTMA 529, the student still owns the account.

This means the student retains full control of the money at the age of majority.

So yes, if they decide that spring break in Cancun sounds more fun than tuition, they can make that choice. They may owe taxes and penalties, but nothing is stopping them.

In theory, particularly for FAFSA schools, a UTMA 529 may be treated more favorably than a standard UTMA investment account.

In practice, I have not found this to be a particularly effective solution.

I have seen these accounts create confusion, control issues, and ultimately fail to deliver enough benefit to justify the complications.

It might make sense if:

- The account has substantial gains
- Selling would create a significant tax issue
- The money will be used for education
- The family is comfortable with the student eventually controlling it

Your tax professional can advise on that.

But in most cases, I am not particularly enthusiastic about this move.

Checking, Savings & Brokerage Accounts

Student-held checking, savings, and brokerage accounts can also be problematic because of the heavier weighting schools assign to them.

That said, balances matter.

If a student has a small trading account with $1,000 or $2,000 because they became interested in stocks, that's usually not the biggest issue.

But context matters.

The single mom I mentioned earlier was so close to the Cal Grant ceiling that every dollar counted.

I see a few situations like that every year.

So while a small student account is not usually disastrous, it can become important when viewed in the context of the family's full financial picture.

If a student has been saving for a car and has $5,000 or $10,000 in an account in their name, that money can work against them.

In such a case, I usually suggest one of two things:

- Buy the car sooner rather than later; or
- Add a parent, grandparent, other relative, or trusted person to the account—and no, not a high school sweetheart—or transfer it altogether.

Since I just brought up spending the money, I'll explain this in a bit more detail.

Spend the Asset

I told you some of these strategies would be easy.

What is easier—or more fun—than spending money on something you wanted or needed anyway?

Sometimes families have unusually large account balances because the money has already been earmarked for a future project.

One of the students I'm working with—recently accepted to both Berkeley and UCLA—had a mom who kept a large savings balance because she was planning major home renovations.

Like so many of us, she had every intention of getting started… and life just kept getting in the way.

When I first saw the asset, I assumed we would need a much more complicated strategy.

We didn't.

The strategy was simply to move forward with the project and spend the money as she had already planned.

Have you been thinking about replacing the roof, but telling yourself it can probably wait another five years?

Consider moving the timeline up if reducing your reported assets by $25,000 to $30,000 improves your aid picture.

Here is the irony:
Parents often assume the only way to afford college is to save every dollar, keep the old car running forever, and avoid spending.

But sometimes the opposite is true.

Sometimes families save money on college by spending money on legitimate needs.

We are not trying to cheat the system.

We are using the system intelligently because we understand how it works.

And yes, sometimes this can work even close to the filing date.

I do not tell families to play games.

But there have certainly been situations where a family knew the money was already committed, the work was already underway, and the asset would be gone by the time the school reviewed the file.

For example, I had a family installing solar panels and battery backup. The permits caused a slight delay, but the project was already in motion well before a school would typically inquire.

Just keep this in mind: schools do audit, and you need to be able to explain what happened.

Other "Spend the Asset" Ideas

Retail therapy is not the strategy — although I understand the appeal.

Here are some legitimate ways families use assets they were already going to spend anyway.

The key phrase here is "money you were already going to spend anyway."

This is not about inventing expenses.

It is about timing legitimate expenses thoughtfully.

UTMA/UGMA Accounts

- Computer
- Summer programs
- Sports
- Tutoring
- Camps
- Car, in some cases

- Travel for school visits

I especially like school visits because they offer a dual benefit: you reduce a problematic asset and help your student make a better college decision.

Other Liquid Accounts

- Pay down credit cards
- Pay down car loans
- Home repairs
- Medical or dental work
- Business equipment
- Necessary household expenses
- Prepay certain expenses
- Move money into retirement, subject to limits and caveats
- Move money into the business
- Purchase needed items for the student
- Replace an old car
- Home improvements
- School visits
- A much-needed vacation

Other Details About Spending Assets

"What about paying down or paying off my house?"

This is a common question.

The FAFSA does not count the equity in your primary residence.

But some CSS schools do.

Philosophically, I generally advise against locking up liquid money in a house if it means sacrificing flexibility.

"What about paying down my rental?"

That can backfire because you are often just moving money from one pocket to another, and the school may still treat that equity as available.

"I'll just contribute more to retirement."

Maybe.

But be careful.

Some schools will add those retirement contributions back to your income, so while the asset might be moved into a more favorable category, the income side may worsen.

Add or Change the Owner

Earlier, I said that some of these strategies are as simple as a phone call and a signature.

This is exactly what I meant.

In many cases, bank accounts only require the current and new account holders to present identification.

If you have a broker, they may handle it for you.

If the account is online-only, it may take a little longer, but the process can still be simple.

Why do we care?

If a parent is a joint owner, the asset may now be treated as a parent asset rather than a student asset.

That can change the weighting dramatically.

As I mentioned earlier, sometimes someone other than a parent may be a more appropriate owner.

Since financial aid forms generally focus on parent and student assets, transferring ownership outside that circle may change what must be reported.

One thing to keep in mind: the CSS Profile often asks whether any other relative plans to contribute to the student's college costs.

That question is very specific.

It is not asking whether Grandma has some money saved.

It is asking whether someone else plans to help with college.

And the truth is, that can be hard to know.

Family dynamics change. Economies change. Promises change.

At a minimum, adding a joint owner can sometimes help.

If appropriate, changing the owner altogether may be more beneficial.

This is not something to be done casually.

Changing ownership can have tax, legal, and family consequences, so this is an area where you should consult your CPA, financial advisor, or attorney before making any changes.

Final Thoughts on Timing & Positioning Strategies

In many cases, the fastest asset strategies are not the most complicated.

They begin with ownership.

Who owns the asset? How is it titled?

Then, can it be spent on something legitimate before the forms are filed? Or repositioned without creating a bigger problem elsewhere?

Those questions matter more than most families realize.

But once we move into 529 plans, rental properties, and insurance-based planning, the strategy becomes more nuanced.

That is where we are headed next.

23

Advanced Asset Strategies

Some asset strategies are simple and may involve little more than a call, a form, and a signature.

Others require more time, planning, documentation, and sometimes assistance from a professional.

That chapter focuses on the more advanced strategies.

Those that require more planning but can make a meaningful difference when executed correctly.

529 Plans

We have discussed 529 plans extensively in this book, and now it's time to explore how to use them strategically.

The first thing to remember is that a 529 plan has two important parties:

- The owner
- The beneficiary

The owner is the person who opened and controls the account, usually a parent.

The beneficiary is the student designated to use the money for qualified education expenses.

If money is withdrawn for non-qualified expenses, the earnings may be subject to taxes and penalties. The original contributions are not taxed because they were made with after-tax dollars.

Ownership Matters

In most cases, the account balance is counted as part of the owner's assets, not the beneficiary's.

That is why simply changing the beneficiary usually does not resolve the issue.

Recent FAFSA changes have also made student-owned 529 plans for dependent students less of a concern than before, but ownership still matters significantly.

For practical purposes, there are two major 529 categories worth discussing:

- 529s owned by a non-parent
- 529s owned by a parent

There are other variations, and plans vary by state and provider. I will not attempt to catalog every possible version in this book.

Some plans allow certain strategies; others do not.

If you call your plan administrator and a strategy isn't available, don't be discouraged. Focus on the next option you can control.

Non-Parent-Owned 529 Plans

When a 529 is owned by someone other than a parent — a grandparent, aunt, uncle, or trusted friend — it generally is not counted as a parent or student asset on the FAFSA.

That can be a significant advantage.

On the CSS Profile, however, schools often inquire about assets set aside for education by other individuals.

That question deserves careful consideration.

As I've mentioned before, family dynamics change.

Are you absolutely certain that the money will be used for the student?

Is there any chance the owner might decide to use it for something else, even if doing so would trigger taxes and penalties?

We have also seen cases where the family had no idea a grandparent or other relative had opened the account.

Parent-Owned Plans

This is the most common setup: a parent-owned account with the child as the beneficiary.

These accounts are counted as parent assets.

One crucial point is that schools look at the total balance by owner, not by child.

So if you have multiple 529 accounts for multiple kids, the total still belongs to the same owner.

A father with three boys attended one of my workshops.

During the workshop, I mentioned that balances under about $40,000 are often not a major issue.

He looked relieved and told me that none of his balances were over $30,000.

I asked, "Balances?"

He said, "I have $30,000 for each boy, so I'm fine because my oldest doesn't have a huge account."

I had to break it to him:
"That's still $90,000 of parent-owned 529 assets on your oldest son's financial aid form."

He immediately said, "What if I change the beneficiary to one of the younger ones?"

Still $90,000.

That was a shock.

We subsequently worked together, and in his case, we were able to get the full amount excluded from consideration. His son received an excellent offer from USC.

The strategy was not changing the beneficiary.

It was changing the owner.

In California, and with most plans I've encountered, that is often possible.

You usually need to call the plan administrator or broker and ask specifically whether an ownership change is allowed.

And fair warning: the person you first talk to may not know.

If the plan allows it, the good news is that an ownership change often does not create a tax problem.

Just give it time. These changes can take a few weeks.

What if your plan doesn't allow for an ownership change?

You still have options:

Transfer to another plan
Move on
Liquidate and take the tax hit

Spend it down

Transfer to another plan

Sometimes the issue is not state law; it is simply the provider.

I worked with a single mom and a helpful family member. They had to transfer the account to another plan first, then change the ownership. It took about six weeks, but the result was worth it.

Move On

Sometimes the juice isn't worth the squeeze. Not every strategy deserves your time.

Liquidate and Take the Tax Hit

Sometimes this is absolutely the right move.

I worked with a single father who took about a $6,000 tax hit by liquidating a 529. In exchange, he gained roughly $18,000 per year in aid.

Paying $6,000 in taxes to gain $72,000 over four years was a very good trade.

Spend it Down

Rules regarding qualified education expenses have loosened in recent years.

We have seen families use 529 funds for K–12 tuition, tutoring, or private school classes for grade remediation or to fulfill missing requirements.

Sometimes the simplest answer is to use the money.

Student-Owned 529 Plans

As I mentioned earlier, dependent student-owned 529 plans are now generally treated more like parent assets for FAFSA purposes.

That's the good news.

The bad news is that the student owns the money.

And yes, I have seen students use those funds for things other than education.

Sometimes, at 19 or 20 years old, taxes and penalties don't feel as real compared to immediate gratification.

Epic spring break in Cabo... 2 AM tacos... You get the idea.

Proceed with caution.

Insurance Products as a Tool

Some families choose to hold part of their long-term savings in insurance-based products rather than in traditional college savings accounts or taxable investment accounts.

Why?

Because certain **properly structured** insurance products may be **excluded from financial aid asset calculations** while still allowing the family to build accessible value over time.

In some cases, a family may later borrow against the cash value of those policies to help fund education expenses, often on more favorable terms than other borrowing options.

These strategies may also carry tax advantages depending on how they are structured and used.

I have referred families to licensed professionals who helped them implement insurance-based strategies that meaningfully improved both their financial aid positioning and their long-term retirement outlook.

Insurance products can be powerful tools in the right situation and costly mistakes in the wrong one.

They can involve fees, surrender periods, complexity, and long-term commitments.

The key is not the product itself, but whether it fits your broader financial plan.

A Word About Annuities

You may also hear advisors recommend annuities as part of financial aid planning.

While sometimes useful, they are often oversold.

Like insurance products generally, annuities are not inherently good or bad. They are tools.

The right product for one family may be the wrong one for another.

If an advisor immediately recommends an annuity or insurance product without first understanding your full financial picture, retirement goals, liquidity needs, and college funding timeline, that should raise a red flag.

Work with professionals who understand both the product and the larger strategy.

Because insurance and annuity products are regulated financial tools, families should work with a properly licensed professional before implementing any of these strategies.

These can be powerful in the right situation—and costly mistakes in the wrong one.

The key is not the product, but whether it fits your overall plan.

Rental Property

Rental properties warrant their own section due to the significant impact they can have on financial aid.

Schools count the equity in rental properties when calculating financial aid.

I work with families on two primary strategies concerning rental properties, each of which we'll break down:

- Valuation
- Equity positioning

Valuation

This is a high-impact strategy that often takes very little effort beyond disciplined thinking.

Many families overvalue their rental properties.

That makes sense. In most areas of life, we want our assets to appear as valuable as possible.

But when it comes to financial aid forms, you want to be realistic.

The rule of thumb I use is simple:
What could you sell this property for if you had to sell it this week, as-is?

No new paint. No fresh carpet. No cleanup. No repair budget. No pretending the roof has another decade left.

And do not forget about commissions and transaction costs.

When families think about it that way, it is not unusual to see the real number drop by 20% or more.

And yes, I know.

"But Zillow says..."

Zillow is great for dinner conversations.

This is not that kind of valuation.

Use a realistic, defensible number.

Overvaluing a property by tens of thousands of dollars can absolutely hurt you.

Equity Positioning

If you still have meaningful equity even after being realistic about value, it may be time to consider how that equity is positioned.

The three strategies I most commonly discuss here are:

- Active business conversion
- Equity stripping
- Bonus depreciation via cost segregation

There are other strategies, but many are too niche to be helpful in a book like this.

Active Business Conversion

This strategy involves converting a rental from a passive investment into an active business.

That generally requires providing and documenting significant services and materially participating in the activity—not just collecting checks.

A common benchmark is roughly 750 hours of material participation per year, properly documented.

Why do this?

Because under the 2025 law changes, moving the rental into a qualifying business structure may help remove it from FAFSA asset consideration if the business has fewer than 100 employees.

What is the downside?

Lenders do not always favor this.

Sometimes changing the title or structure can trigger loan issues or force a refinance conversation.

In some cases, a lender will give written consent, and everything proceeds smoothly.

This can work well, but it requires documentation and lender coordination.

Equity Stripping

Terrible name. Very real strategy.

The basic idea is to reduce the amount of exposed equity by taking on debt against the property, then moving the proceeds into an asset that is treated more favorably for financial aid purposes.

That second step often involves an insurance product or annuity, though not always.

A family might work with a lender to place a first or second mortgage on the rental property or, in some cases, document an intrafamily lien.

Then the proceeds are repositioned.

This is not a senior-year strategy.

Ideally, this happens in the student's freshman or sophomore year of high school.

If a CSS school sees a new mortgage that suddenly wipes out visible equity, it may exercise professional judgment and add the equity back.

This must be done for legitimate financial reasons and properly documented.

If it appears to be a last-minute move solely to reduce aid eligibility, schools may push back.

Bonus Depreciation

This usually means either purchasing a new rental property or performing a cost segregation study on an existing one.

A cost segregation study is a detailed engineering-style analysis that identifies components of a property—such as lighting, carpeting, appliances, and landscaping—that can be depreciated faster than the building itself.

This allows depreciation to be accelerated into the college-planning years.

Why does that matter?

Because it can create a significant paper loss, which may reduce AGI and improve the family's aid position.

I worked with a family whose AGI was just over $900,000.

They had several rental properties and substantial liquid assets.

Using cost segregation combined with equity positioning dramatically improved their financial aid standing.

It took nearly a year to implement properly.

This brings us back to the theme:

Start early.

These are powerful tools, but they need to be implemented correctly and with the help of professionals with proven expertise.

Final Thoughts on Complex Assets

As powerful as these strategies can be, they all share one thing in common:

They work best when implemented early, properly documented, and aligned with your overall financial picture.

This brings us to one of the most important themes of this entire book:

Timing.

24

Timing, Documentation & Credibility

Occasionally, I hear a family say something like:

"Oh, we don't have much income, so it sounds like we have time to deal with the assets."

I understand the logic.

But please be cautious.

Some strategies are simple.

Others require time, coordination, and documentation.

And that difference matters more than most families expect.

The more complex your situation—such as large portfolios, layered ownership, real estate, business interests, or tax issues—the longer these strategies take to implement effectively.

For example, if a family decides to stop contributing to a 529 plan and redirect savings into another vehicle, the earlier they do so, the better the results.

Waiting until senior year rarely gives those strategies enough time to work.

The earlier you start, the more options you have.

The later you start, the fewer options remain.

A Word for Those Who Might Be Behind Schedule

If you are reading this as a parent of a senior, do not panic.

You're not too late—you're just working with a shorter runway.

Some of these strategies can still be effective.

I also understand that life happens.

One of our children changed direction midway through senior year.

It happens.

You adjust.

If you have the luxury of time, I recommend starting in the ninth or tenth grade.

But the second-best time to start is now.

Asset Timing

I have mentioned timing throughout the book, but this is where it becomes particularly important.

Assets are recorded as of the day you submit the FAFSA or CSS Profile.

That sounds simple.

But waiting too long can raise questions.

My good friend, Ron—whom some people call the Godfather of College Planning—likes to remind families that colleges are old institutions. They have been examining financial statements and family situations for a very long time.

He is right.

Financial aid offices handle millions of dollars every year.

They have seen these strategies before.

"The School Can't Unsee an Asset"

I say this to families all the time:

The school can't unsee an asset.

No, it's not grammatically perfect.

But it is true.

Once a school sees an asset, it becomes much harder to explain its later disappearance.

None of the strategies we've discussed is inherently improper.

But context matters.

Schools can—and do—apply professional judgment.

If something looks like a last-minute move purely to improve aid eligibility, they may adjust the numbers.

If the move happened in junior year or earlier, schools are generally much less suspicious.

Last-minute moves sometimes work.
But they are more likely to draw scrutiny.

And yes, in a significant percentage of cases, schools will ask for documentation.

That does not mean you are in trouble.

It just means you need paperwork and a reasonable explanation.

Timing Estimates

Not all strategies are created equal.

Some can be executed in a few days.

Others take months—and sometimes close to a year—to implement properly.

Here's a rough guide:

Strategy	Time to Execute	Recommended Timing
Add a joint account holder	Hours to days	Junior year or earlier; can sometimes still be done late
Change owner	Days	Junior year or earlier; can sometimes still be done late
529 owner change	Weeks	Junior year is ideal; early senior year may still work
Property valuation adjustment	Hours	Any time before filing, as long as it is supportable
Business Conversion	6 Months +	Sophomore year is ideal; junior year may still be workable
Equity Stripping	3 - 6 Months	Sophomore year is ideal; junior year may still be workable
Cost Segregation/Bonus Depreciation	9-12 Months	Freshman or sophomore year is best

Some strategies can happen quickly. Others require months of planning—which is why starting early matters so much.

The point is not that these timelines are exact.

The point is that the time to execute on strategies can vary significantly.

"What If I Don't Report It?" or "How Will They Know?"

I get this question from time to time.

It is usually a signal to me that we need to slow down and talk through the risks.

It can feel like a school would never know about an asset unless you provided it with the statement.

But often they do not need the statement to know something is there.

Not long ago, I had a client who left a significant asset off our intake form.

When I reviewed the tax return, I noticed a very large number on the ordinary dividends line.

That was one of several clues.

On our next call, I asked about the multimillion-dollar account for which I did not have a statement.

There was a long pause.

Then the husband asked, "How did you know about that account?"

I'm not an accountant.

But if I can spot clues like that, a financial aid office certainly can.

The same is true for rental property income showing up on Schedule E.

And if you are wondering whether you can simply "forget" to disclose an asset, my answer is simple:

Do not do that.

We have seen situations—especially at faith-based schools—where not only was aid rescinded, but acceptance as well.

It is not worth it.

Not even close.

Final Thoughts: You Can Do Everything Right... and Still Overpay

By now, you've probably realized something important:

There is a lot you can control.

How your income appears.
When you make key decisions.
How your assets are positioned.

How well you document your situation.

All of that matters.

And if done well, it can significantly improve your financial aid outcome.

But there is another truth that I want you to understand before we move on:

You can do everything right…
…and still end up with a disappointing offer.

Not because you made a mistake.

Not because you missed something.

But because of one factor we haven't fully explored yet:

The school you choose.

Financial aid is not just about how your family looks on paper.

It is also about **how a school chooses to respond** to that information.

Some schools have the resources and the willingness to be generous.

Others simply do not.

And that can be the difference between stressing over every payment or continuing to plan for retirement.

In the next chapter, we're going to talk about one of the most overlooked—and most powerful—parts of this entire process:

School selection.

Or more specifically:

Finding schools that have money—and are willing to use it.

25

School Selection

"Why not Duke? It's just down the street from your house."

"There is no way we could afford that."

This is how a conversation began with a mom whose daughter was considering a few HBCU schools—primarily because she assumed they would be more affordable.

I'll come back to that story in a moment.

But first, I want to introduce a concept that changes everything when it comes to financial aid:

You don't get aid because you need it.
You get aid because the school can—and wants—to give it.

And that is a very different system than most families realize.

School Financial Aid Dynamics

I'll break schools into four broad categories.

Thinking about them this way makes the financial aid picture much easier to understand:

- Schools with limited aid resources
- Schools that can pay... but don't have to
- Schools that compete with generosity
- Schools that use aid strategically

Oversimplified?

A little.

But this framework will make the entire financial aid landscape much easier to understand.

So let's walk through what I mean.

Schools With Limited Aid Resources

Do you remember Dominic's memorable (horrible) saying from earlier in the book?

"You can't borrow money from your broke friends, so don't try to get money from a school that doesn't have any."

I hate to admit it... but he's right.

Some colleges simply do not have much money to share with students.

That does not mean they have no money at all.

It means the pool is small, and only a limited number of students will receive a portion.

The student mentioned at the beginning of this chapter is one example.

She was looking at several HBCUs.

These can provide wonderful educational experiences and may offer tremendous academic, cultural, and social benefits.

However, in my experience, many of these schools have historically offered less financial aid than larger, well-endowed institutions.

The good news is that this has begun to change in some cases, thanks to successful alumni increasing their donations.

And of course, HBCUs are not the only schools in this category.

Schools with smaller endowments—often under $100 million—may simply not be able to offer every student a generous financial aid package.

Schools That Can Pay... But Don't Have To

In 2025, there were some very public arguments between the government and colleges over this exact issue: schools with tens of billions of dollars in endowment assets spending relatively little on student financial aid.

To be fair, it is a mistake to think of a school's endowment as a giant financial aid checking account.

Much of that money is restricted.

A donor might give $5 million and specify that it can only be used for cancer research or medical equipment.

Endowments are also often invested in long-term assets, so the school typically spends earnings rather than the principal itself.

That is true of wealthy schools across the board.

What differs, however, is institutional policy.

Some wealthy schools are highly generous.

Others are not.

The less generous schools can afford not to be.

They attract enough strong applicants and full-pay families that they do not need to spend aggressively to fill their classes.

They may offer some merit awards to attract highly desired students, but overall, they are in a position to preserve their resources and still attract excellent applicants.

They don't need to compete on price.

So often… they don't.

Schools That Compete with Generosity

These schools may also have large endowments and the same donation restrictions.

But they take a different approach.

They use financial aid aggressively to attract desired students.

Because of that generosity, their schools become more desirable.

That, in turn, allows them to be increasingly selective.

And that often creates a cycle of:

Improved reputation
Successful graduates
Stronger alumni support
Future endowment growth

It's not charity.

It's a strategy.

When you step back, both approaches make sense from the school's perspective.

But one is obviously much better for your family.

Schools That Use Aid Strategically

Then there is another very important category.

These are often schools with moderate endowments—perhaps in the $300 million to $500 million range—that are not necessarily household names but still offer an excellent education.

Because they are not as well-known, they often need to work harder to attract strong students.

So they use money strategically.

They may offer very competitive packages because they would rather collect some tuition than none at all.

These schools are often among the most interesting to identify because they may not look exciting at first glance, but they can be game changers financially.

How Do You Know?

At this point, most parents ask the same question:

"How do I actually figure this out?"

When you were applying to college, you may remember a large book called *Peterson's College Guide*.

That company is still around and offers helpful tools.

A large part of their business today involves selling data to professionals like me, enabling us to assist families.

But that does not mean you are out of options.

There are several effective ways to research this:

- Research tools such as Google and AI platforms like ChatGPT
- College fairs and virtual seminars
- College visits

Let's discuss each of these.

Research Tools Such as Google & AI Platforms

This seems obvious, but what families often overlook is the need to search for specific information—and then verify it.

If you search, "What does UT Austin cost?" you'll only find limited information.

Much of what you find will be paid search results or marketing copy from the school itself.

That may lead you to a Net Price Calculator or a general financial aid page, but it still leaves you with more questions than answers.

This is where specific searches become useful.

Recall that earlier in the book, I provided three of the most important questions to ask about a school:

- How much need do they meet?
- How much of that is free money?
- How long, on average, does it take to graduate?

If you search for those answers—along with the school's cost of attendance and endowment size—you'll be much closer to understanding how that school truly approaches financial aid.

For example, if you see a very large endowment paired with a relatively low percentage of need met, that may indicate a wealthy school that simply chooses not to be very generous.

I also see parents make the mistake of trusting the first answer they get from an AI tool.

AI tools are useful.

But they can also provide outdated information.

So make sure to ask for information relevant to the current year—or the years your student will be in college.

Then check it against another source.

Or, better yet, ask the AI tool to show its sources.

These small habits can make a big difference.

College Fairs & Online Seminars

You know the expression: "Go straight to the horse's mouth"?

This is one of those situations.

College fairs and school-hosted financial aid seminars are powerful learning opportunities.

Do they take time you don't have? Yep.
Are they boring? Often.
Are they worth it? 100%.

Each offers an opportunity to ask someone at the school direct questions about financial aid.

I always tell parents to do some homework before attending.

Research the school first.

Write down your questions.

Be prepared.

And if what they say contradicts what you found in your research, ask them about it.

In the next chapter, I'm going to discuss another reason these things matter.

But for now, simply know this:
If you show up prepared, these events can be worth their weight in gold.

College Visits

I want to emphasize the importance of visiting schools.

Are visits an added expense? Yes.
Are they worth it? 1000%.

When you visit, you can often make an appointment to meet with a financial aid representative.

Do schools claim those visits don't influence aid?

Yes.

Have I seen them matter anyway?

Countless times.

But even if they had no effect on your aid, they still matter.

You may need to call the school later for clarification or an appeal.

Isn't it nice to have a face to go with the name?

You can also discuss your hypothetical situation and gain a much better sense of what they would need if questions arise.

That alone can save a significant amount of time.

And what about the cost?

Some visits may require just a one-day drive.

Others may necessitate a flight and a hotel.

But do you know one of the most expensive things that can happen in your student's college career?

"Mom. I hate this place so much."

Yep. Changing schools.

They saw the pictures.
They heard the stories.

Their friends are going there.

Then they arrive…

And hate it.

The neighborhood is expensive.
It's too hot or too cold.
There's nothing to do.
It's too much of a party school.

Changing schools will cost you far more than the plane ticket and hotel ever will.

Merit vs. Need

We've discussed this distinction earlier in the book, but now that we're talking about school selection, it's worth revisiting.

Generally, when I refer to aid, I mean anything that helps lower the cost of college.

I love all of it.

But strategically, merit and need-based aid are different.

Need-based aid starts with math.

COA - SAI = Need

This calculation yields a number.

How much of that need the school actually meets depends on the school's policies.

A large share of that institutional aid often comes from the school's own resources.

So yes, a family could receive little or no federal aid and still get a very large institutional need-based package from the school.

If a school meets 100% of need, it covers the full amount.

If it meets 60%, you are responsible for the gap.

Merit aid is different.

Here is one of the biggest takeaways in this chapter:

Merit aid is often not a separate pot of money.
It is a tuition discount.

A price adjustment... not a reward.

Schools use merit to determine a number they think your family can pay—and to attract students they want.

That is why schools that need to compete tend to use merit more aggressively than those that don't.

Seller schools are rarely under pressure to discount heavily.

Students already want to go there.

This is why much of this chapter focuses on identifying schools that effectively use both need and merit to your advantage.

Need-Blind vs. Need-Aware

Your finances can also affect your student's chances of admission.

A simple way to think about it is this:

Need-blind:
The admissions office does not consider the family's ability to pay when deciding whether to admit the student.

Need-aware:
The school does consider financial need, especially when making decisions at the margin.

If two students are close, and the school is down to a handful of spots, a need-aware school may favor the student who can pay full price.

That is worth knowing as you research schools.

You usually won't find this stated very clearly on a school website, but you can often get a sense of it from a school's reputation, direct conversations, and, yes, careful online research.

Building a School List

I know this chapter is a lot to digest.

Choosing the right school can feel as easy as predicting your teenager's mood from one day to the next.

And you're not entirely wrong.

Schools can shift from one category to another over time—or even during a single admissions cycle—depending on finances and enrollment needs.

Still, the main takeaway is this:

Building a school list is about balance.

I see well-intentioned families tell their student to build a "dream school" list, promising they'll figure it out later.

That's a beautiful sentiment.

It's just not always practical.

On the other side, I see families select only schools that seem "cheap."

That can be equally as limiting.

What I suggest is building a list around three criteria.

Dominic calls it the **Triad of Economics & Admissions—TEA.**

He's British and a marketing guy. Can you tell?

He's very proud of it.

The three criteria are:

Acceptance: Your student has a reasonable chance of getting in.
Fit: The school fits the student academically, socially, and personally.
Affordability: The school is affordable either at face value or through aid.

That is how you build a list that works for your student, your family, and your finances.

Acceptance

Typically, schools are broken down into three admissions categories:

Safety (Likely):

GPA and test scores are in the 75th percentile or better, with admission rates of 50% or higher, and crucially, they are **financially affordable.**

Target (Match):

GPA and test scores are in the middle 50%, with admission rates of roughly 30%–50%.

Reach (Long Shot):

GPA and test scores are in the lower 25%, or the school has an admission rate under 30%.

Technically, any school with an admission rate under 20% is a reach for everyone.

In most cases, the bulk of a student's list should be in the target range.

Your admissions professional can guide you more specifically, but a rough distribution might look like this:

- 2–3 safety schools
- 4–5 target schools
- 2–3 reach schools

Fit

A few years ago, a mother wanted to work with me.

She told me her son needed to transfer to an Ivy League school.

He was already attending Chapman University—a small but highly respected school in Orange County, California.

So I asked:

"Does he want to transfer?"
"No, he loves Chapman and is doing really well."
"So why the move?"
"Because my son will go to an Ivy League."

I ultimately told her we weren't a good fit.

I wish that were an isolated case.

I have seen plenty of parents dictate where their child will go.

Family pride. Ego. Bragging rights. Alumni ties.

Whatever the reason, the student's actual comfort and preferences are often overlooked.

To each their own… but I wouldn't recommend it.

However, I highly recommend considering the student's comfort.

This is something you can work through with a counselor or admissions expert, but please don't ignore it.

Affordability

This is where everything we've discussed in this book comes together.

How to Build It

I'll use the funnel illustration again.

Start broad.

Then narrow intentionally.

If you are working with an admissions expert or counselor, they usually focus on two of the three TEA criteria:

- Acceptance
- Fit

What they often don't fully understand is the financial side.

One of my favorite clients is a mom in the Midwest.

She has worked for several years with a well-known college advising company.

They have done a great job identifying schools based on admissions and fit.

Each time the list changes, she sends it to me, and I run the schools through our database to assess affordability.

You can do something similar without expensive databases by using the research methods we discussed earlier in this chapter.

Stay in contact with your student and their counselor.

Get updated lists as things change.

Then do the financial research.

You'll usually see quickly which schools are a financial fit and which are not.

Just make sure you don't overload the list with dream schools.

As with most things in life, balance is key.

School Selection: Final Thoughts

This is a meaty topic because it has a meaningful impact on financial aid.

When I meet with families who already have a senior—or even a student in college—they are often mystified about why they are paying so much, despite their income and assets not appearing particularly high.

Ninety-nine percent of the time, school selection is the issue.

In fact, about a week before starting this book, I met with a mom who was in exactly that situation.

They had generous offers from multiple schools.

Their income and assets were modest and not particularly detrimental to their financial aid eligibility.

But at the last minute, their daughter decided to attend a very popular out-of-state public school.

They assumed they could just add the school to the FAFSA and let the system work.

They received $0.

Not "less than expected."

Zero.

And to make matters worse, the daughter hated it there and wanted to come home.

So, whether you remember Dominic's "broke friend" analogy, his TEA acronym, or simply the idea that affordability needs to be part of the school list from the beginning, just don't forget this:

School selection doesn't just influence financial aid.
In many cases, it determines it.

But there's another layer to this.

Even within the right schools…
Even when the money is available…
Not every student receives the same offer.

Why?

Because schools aren't just evaluating your finances.

They're evaluating your student.

In the next chapter, we'll discuss one of the most overlooked ways families improve their outcomes:

How your student's direction, interests, and positioning can influence both admissions and the money that follows.

26

Direction Creates Opportunity

At some point in almost every conversation, a parent will say:

"We'll just make up the difference with scholarships."

I understand why that feels like a plan.

But in reality, most families approach scholarships backward.

They start with the money.
They search online.
They apply to anything they can find.
They hope something hits.

But scholarships, admissions strength, and even some department-level funding often become much more attainable when they start somewhere else:

With direction.

Not a perfect career plan.

Not asking your student to decide their entire future at 15.

Just a direction.

Because direction creates experience.

Experience creates a story.

And a story creates opportunity.

Student Positioning

Up to this point, we've focused heavily on institutional strategy:

Income.
Assets.
Timing.
School selection.

That's about putting your family in the best possible position.

But there is another layer:

Your student's position.

This includes their direction, experiences, interests, and story.

You've probably heard about this in the context of admissions.

But it can also influence funding.

And one of the most overlooked parts of this is something many parents find uncomfortable:
Choosing a direction early.

Directional Accuracy (Not Perfection)

I am a mom of three.

I am not asking your child to decide their entire career at 15.

That's unrealistic.

And unnecessary.

What is realistic is something we call:

Directional accuracy.

Not a detailed life plan, but just a general sense of direction.

Because having a direction—even a tentative one—creates opportunities that simply don't exist otherwise.

Why Direction Matters

There are two major advantages to having some direction early.

Experience Advantage

When a student has direction, even a loose one, they can start exploring it through:

Internships
Job shadowing
Volunteering
Conversations with people in the field

And this almost always leads to a positive outcome.

Why do I say that so confidently?

Because I tell parents this:

If they love it, that's a win.
If they hate it, that's also a win.

We've had students who were convinced they wanted to be dentists…

Until they spent a day looking inside people's mouths.

That was the end of that.

And that is a win.

Because it's far better to figure that out at 16 than halfway through a very expensive degree.

Financial Advantage

This is the part most families overlook.

When a student has direction, they may gain access to:

- Department-level scholarships
- Program-specific funding
- Opportunities tied to a field of study

One of my favorite moments in a workshop came from a mom in the audience.

She raised her hand and said:

> I wish I had met y'all sooner. Everything you're saying is true. We got way more money from private schools than from public schools. But we later found out we could have gotten even more. My daughter went in undeclared—and there was another $15,000 available if she had just declared her major.

That's not uncommon.

General applicants compete with everyone.

Students with direction often compete in smaller, more targeted pools.

A Real-Life Example (and a Parenting Reality Check)

I'll give you a quick example from our own home.

Our daughter was accidentally enrolled in a medical terminology class in high school.

She planned to drop it.

But she loved it.

She took the advanced version the next year.

So Dominic suggested, “Why don’t you look at something in the medical field?”

She wasn’t interested.

A couple of weeks later, she sat down with our business partner, whom she calls Uncle Ron.

At dinner that night, she was excited to tell us she had decided to pursue something in the medical field.

That’s directional accuracy.

Dominic mistakenly said, "That's what I told you."

To which she replied, without missing a beat:

“No, you didn’t.”

If you’re a parent, you already know how that conversation felt.

These conversations aren’t always easy.

But they matter.

How to Start Exploring Direction

This doesn’t have to be complicated.

Start with simple questions:

What subjects do you enjoy?
What kinds of problems interest you?
What do you think you might want to try?

Then go one step deeper.

I recently worked with a student who said, “I really like theater.”

“Great. Tell me more. Have you acted?”

“I played a background character, which was fun. Then I worked with the tech crew, and that was awesome. I also did costumes and makeup.”

"Which part did you enjoy most?"

"I loved building the sets."

That's the direction.

Is she committed to being a set designer for life? No.

But is she moving toward something creative and hands-on, potentially behind the scenes in theater or film?

Absolutely.

That's directional accuracy.

Then take it one step further:

Talk to friends or neighbors in those fields.
Ask about shadowing opportunities.
Offer to help, volunteer, or learn.
Even offering unpaid help—where appropriate—is often just a signal of commitment.

You're not locking in a career.

You're helping your student gather information.

And that information becomes incredibly valuable later.

And this is where scholarships re-enter the conversation.

Because once a student has direction, scholarships stop being a random internet search.

They become targeted.

Where Scholarships Actually Fit

Now that we have that direction in mind, it's time to talk about scholarships.

Scholarships can absolutely help.

But they are rarely the foundation of affordability.

Most are:

- Smaller
- More targeted
- Tied to something specific

Which is why direction matters.

A student applying randomly is competing against everyone.

A student with a clear direction, relevant experiences, and a story that fits the opportunity is often competing in a much smaller pool.

How To Think About This

Instead of asking:
"What scholarships can we find?"

A better question is:
"What opportunities does this student naturally align with?"

That shift alone can change the entire outcome.

You may have heard the expression:

"The riches are in the niches."

Scholarships often work the same way.

A highly specific scholarship—one tied to a particular background, interest, or field—will naturally have a smaller pool of applicants.

Compare that to a national scholarship with over 100,000 applicants competing for a handful of awards.

Which one do you think is more realistic?

We see this play out frequently.

A few years ago, we worked with a student on the autism spectrum.

National scholarships are available—but they are highly competitive.

With a little more targeted research, we found a scholarship specifically for students with autism in a certain part of Southern California.

Much smaller pool.

Much better odds.

We've also seen students receive scholarships based on family background.

One student qualified for funding because her father is a union longshoreman in Los Angeles.

And don't forget the film studies student at USC I mentioned earlier.

That wasn't random.

That was alignment.

These aren't one-off stories.

They are examples of what happens when a student's background, interests, and direction align with the right opportunities.

Direction doesn't guarantee a scholarship.

But it dramatically improves the odds of finding the right ones.

That's when scholarships stop feeling like a lottery…
…and start becoming part of a strategy.

A Quick Note on Process

There is a much deeper system behind finding scholarships, organizing them, and applying effectively.

That's beyond what we can realistically cover in a single chapter.

But if you're the type of parent who appreciates a clear roadmap, we've developed a much more detailed scholarship and positioning system on our website that guides you through the process step by step.

You don't need it to apply what you've learned here.

But if you want structure—and a way to stay consistent—it can be a helpful resource.

Positioning for More: Final Thoughts

If you take nothing else from this chapter, take this:

Direction creates experience.
Experience creates a story.
Story creates opportunity.
And opportunity creates options.

This is true for admissions, scholarships, and department-level funding.

You are not trying to lock your student into a career forever.

You are helping them move from "I have no idea" to "I have a direction worth exploring."

That shift can make a meaningful difference.

Up to this point, we've talked about the intentional choices you make:

The schools you research.
The strategies you implement.
The direction your student explores.

But there is another layer most families overlook:
The things schools learn about you before you ever apply.

27

What Schools Know Before You Apply

When I was younger, I blasted music in my car and sang along to pop songs and EDM.

Now, NPR plays every time I get in my car.

My family often teases me about it.

Apparently, I've reached that stage of life.

But in this case, it's helpful for you.

A few months ago, I was listening to a segment about how colleges are trying to attract more middle-class families—those who can afford to pay at least part of the bill.

During that segment, a brief mention caught my attention:

Colleges are spending millions of dollars to buy data on families.

Dominic comes from a marketing background, so I've heard plenty about how data is used in advertising—and sometimes in ways people don't fully realize.

That got me wondering:

What else are they tracking?

I went down the rabbit hole.

Here's the takeaway:

Schools are not just reading applications.

They are observing behavior.

And in many cases, that behavior is being interpreted long before you ever apply.

You Are Already Being Evaluated

Companies like Google, Meta (Facebook), and even your car collect data about you.

They've become very good at predicting behavior.

Colleges are now tapping into similar tools—using data to better understand prospective students and families.

They're trying to answer questions like:

Do you have a college-bound student?

Where do you live?

What kind of work do you do?

What are your general interests?

They combine that with signals such as:

- Website visits (both on their site and through broader web activity)
- Email engagement
- Event attendance
- Campus visits
- Financial aid seminar participation
- Net Price Calculator usage
- General online behavior and interest patterns inferred from third-party data

Is that a little uncomfortable?

Maybe.

But it's also important to understand what's actually happening here.

Colleges aren't sitting behind a screen watching your every move.

They are using aggregated data—often purchased from third-party providers—to build a general profile of interest, intent, and likelihood to enroll.

In other words:

They're not just seeing what you do on their website.

They're forming a broader picture of you based on how you behave across the internet.

At the end of the day, they're trying to answer one key question:

"Is this student likely to enroll?"

Because enrollment is what ultimately drives revenue.

And that's where this starts to matter for you.

The Mismatch Problem

This is where I began discussing this in workshops and client conversations.

Because sometimes the story your data tells doesn't match your reality.

From the school's perspective, it might look like this:

- The family says they need financial help
- They live in a high-income area
- Their profession suggests strong earnings
- Their behavior reflects high-end interests

But…

- They haven't visited the school
- They haven't attended a financial aid session
- They haven't used the Net Price Calculator
- They haven't engaged with financial aid content

So the question becomes:

How serious are they about this school?
And how much do they actually need?

Now, let's contrast that with reality.

Maybe:

- You rent instead of own
- You're supporting an aging parent
- You haven't taken a real vacation in years
- You like looking at watches but wear an Apple Watch

That's a very different financial picture.

But the data doesn't automatically recognize that.

And that disconnect—between perception and reality—can create friction.

Why This Matters

Colleges are not just evaluating need.

They are deciding where to allocate limited resources.

And like any organization, they are more likely to invest in students who seem engaged and likely to enroll.

That doesn't mean you need to obsess over every click.

But it does mean your behavior sends signals.

Have you:

- Engaged with the school?
- Explored financial aid resources?
- Taken steps that demonstrate genuine interest?

Or did you apply with little to no interaction?

From the school's perspective, those are very different applicants.

Different applicants often receive different outcomes.

Those signals can matter, especially regarding to financial aid decisions.

Not always.

Not at every school.

But often enough that it's worth being intentional.

Practical Behavior Advice

You don't need to change your life.

You just need your behavior to reflect your intent.

Here are a few simple adjustments:

Allow cookies (selectively):
If you're researching a school, allow their site to register that interaction.

Attend events:
Virtual is fine. You don't need to be in the front row taking notes—just show up.

Visit campuses (if possible):
Even one visit can make a difference.

Engage with emails:

You don't need to read everything—but opening and occasionally clicking matters.

Use the Net Price Calculator:
More on that next.

This isn't about gaming the system.

It's about ensuring your behavior reflects your intent.

Net Price Calculators

Net Price Calculators (NPCs) are school-specific tools designed to estimate what a college might cost your family.

Some are excellent.

Some seem like they haven't been updated since 2005.

But they're still useful.

Why They Matter

They signal interest
A factor that matters more than most families realize.

They help with school selection
They aren't perfect—but they're directionally helpful.

They can support future conversations
If your actual offer looks very different, having that earlier estimate can provide useful context.

How to Use Them Effectively

- Take your time and enter accurate information.
- Revisit them if your financial strategy changes.
- Don't overreact to the output—good or bad.

The real value isn't just the number.

It's the combination of:

- Signaling intent.
- Informing your list.
- Creating a reference point.

What Schools Know Before You Apply: Final Thoughts

This isn't the most important lever in the financial aid process.

But it may be one of the easiest to control.

This makes it worth paying attention to.

You don't need to overthink it.

You just need to start early and be intentional.

As data becomes more central to how schools operate, this factor will only become more important over time.

If you have a ninth or tenth grader, you can begin implementing this now—without adding much stress to the process.

28

Before the Offer: Final Thoughts

Over the last several chapters, we've focused on everything that happens before you apply—and before you receive an offer.

While we've examined this from different angles, the core message has been consistent:

Start early.

I know that isn't always possible.

But the earlier you start, the more options you have,
the wider the funnel,
and the more control you keep.

Freshman and sophomore years offer the greatest flexibility.

That's when families can implement longer-term strategies like:

Adjusting income and assets over time
Positioning ownership and investments
Planning around major financial events
Creating opportunities through school selection and student direction

These strategies tend to have the biggest impact—not just on financial aid, but on your overall financial picture.

By junior year, you may still have time—but the margin for error shrinks.

Everything becomes more compressed.

By senior year, your options are often limited to more tactical decisions:

Ownership adjustments
Selective spend-down strategies
Evaluating whether a tax tradeoff is worth the potential aid gain

Those can still work, and for some families, they may be enough.

But there is a clear relationship between complexity and time:

The more complex your situation, the earlier planning matters.

Along the way, we've also expanded the conversation beyond just finances.

Because a strong outcome isn't determined by a single number.

It's influenced by:

Where you apply (school selection)
How your student is positioned (direction, interests, and fit)
What signals you send (engagement, research, and behavior)

Financial aid is not driven by one factor.

It's the result of multiple moving pieces working together.

The strategies in this section are not exhaustive, but they are the ones I have seen work most consistently across the widest range of families.

Of course, not every family starts from a clean, straightforward position.

Some families are navigating divorce.

Others are part of blended families.

Some are remarried.

Some are separated but still living together.

Still, others are dealing with sudden changes in income—up or down.

Some are facing situations that simply don't fit neatly into the boxes the FAFSA and CSS Profile would prefer.

Because here's the reality:

Financial aid formulas are built on tidy assumptions.

Real life rarely is.

So in the next section, we're going to shift from planning in a controlled environment, to navigating what happens when things aren't so clean.

When circumstances change.

When timelines don't cooperate.

When your reality doesn't match the numbers on a form.

In short:

What happens when life gets messy—and how to respond when it does.

PART VI

When Life Gets Messy

Up to this point, much of what we have discussed assumes a fairly straightforward financial picture:

two married parents, stable income, predictable assets, and a household that fits neatly into the boxes the FAFSA and CSS Profile would prefer.

But real life rarely looks that clean.

Families divorce.
Parents remarry.
Households blend.
Income rises.
Income falls.
Businesses have great years and terrible ones.
Relationships change in the middle of the college process.

Sometimes life simply refuses to cooperate with the timing of financial aid formulas.

Unfortunately, the formulas do not care.

They are built on assumptions.

And when your life does not fit those assumptions, things can get complicated quickly.

In this next section, we're going to walk through some of the most common "messy life" situations we see—and how they can affect financial aid.

Because if life is complicated for you right now, you are not alone.

And more importantly:

You are not without options.

29

Divorce, Separation & Financial Aid Reality

Divorce is one of the most emotionally and financially disruptive experiences a family can go through.

And if that is your reality, let me say this clearly:

We understand this is not just a "financial aid strategy" topic.

Dominic has been through a divorce himself and has children from a prior marriage, so this is not theoretical for our family.

We understand, both professionally and personally, that divorce changes everything—your finances, your relationships, your priorities, and yes, your financial aid picture.

It also creates some of the greatest complications in college planning.

About half of the families I work with are in some stage of divorce or separation.

One of the most important things I do is help families separate the emotional reality from the financial aid reality.

Because while every story is different, one thing is almost universal:

Parents assume the college financial aid system will follow common sense or family court logic.

It often does not.

The financial aid system does not consider whether the divorce was amicable, who was "right," or whether one parent is difficult, absent, or unreasonable.

Divorce courts and financial aid offices operate by completely different rulebooks.

That can be a huge surprise.

And it is why divorced families often fall into the same avoidable traps.

Trap #1: Assuming Custody Schedule Determines FAFSA Parent

One of the most common mistakes I see is that families assume the FAFSA parent is simply the parent with the larger share of custody.

That is no longer the rule.

The FAFSA now considers the parent who provided the greater financial support during the 12 months preceding the form's filing.

That means a student could live with Mom all year, but if Dad provided most of the financial support—through child support, car payments, insurance, tuition, or other expenses—then Dad may be the FAFSA parent.

If support is truly equal, the parent with higher income and assets is generally considered.

There is a lot of misinformation out there on this point.

A couple of years ago, when our daughter was a senior, we were on a Zoom call with other senior families to discuss end-of-year events. During the call, the topic of the FAFSA came up, and the counselor said, "You always put the parent the child lives with."

Dominic turned to me and said, "Well, that will probably ruin financial aid for a few people."

He was not wrong.

And this misinformation often reaches students first, especially now that more schools have students complete the FAFSA in class.

The Student's Input

The student starts the FAFSA.

They go to studentaid.gov, create an account, and are prompted to invite the parent who provides the most support.

Personally, I think that's a tough question to ask a teenager.

How are they really supposed to know?

And if custody is split, are they really expected to ask, "Which of you makes more and has more assets?"

But whether I like the question or not, it is the question.

So, if this chapter applies to you, make sure your student knows which parent to select before they start the form.

I am not saying you need to hand them every detail of both households.

I am saying they should not be guessing.

That brings us to the next trap, because many families do not fully understand what "support" actually means.

Trap #2: Misunderstanding What Counts as Support

When the FAFSA refers to "support," it means more than just the mortgage and child support.

Support can include:

- Food
- Clothing
- Car expenses
- Insurance
- Medical costs
- Extracurriculars
- Tuition
- Travel
- Phone
- And much more

In other words, the parent who provides the greater financial support may not be the parent the child lives with most often.

Sometimes it is. Often it is not.

I had a mom whose ex paid substantial child support and was also covering the home she lived in.

He earned much more than she did.

Her immediate assumption was that he must be providing more support.

But when we listed the actual expenses, she was paying for nearly everything else—groceries, insurance, activities, daily costs, and more.

When we added it up, she was actually providing more support than he was.

So we used her information on the FAFSA.

Strategy: Document the Actual Support

One of the best strategies in this situation is simply to figure out what is really happening.

Sometimes the lower-income parent is already covering more of the student's actual expenses—they just haven't stopped to add it up.

I am not encouraging anyone to make something up.

I encourage you to understand the rules well enough to accurately document reality.

The actual support often looks very different once you run the numbers.

And in divorce situations, that can make a meaningful difference in financial aid.

Trap #3: Ignoring College Language in the Divorce/Custody Decree

Earlier, I said that colleges do not really care what your divorce decree says.

That is true, but it does not mean you should ignore it.

I frequently see decrees that require parents to split college costs 50/50.

Sometimes the split mirrors the custody arrangement. Sometimes one parent pays first, and the other reimburses later.

Any of those details can affect the support analysis.

Strategy: Pull Out the Decree and Read It

If you are divorced, locate your decree and review any language related to college.

A sentence buried in that document can materially change your planning.

That does not mean the school is enforcing your decree.

It means the decree may help explain who is expected to provide support and what your real-world support pattern has been.

And that may matter.

The key point is this:

Financial aid offices are not really interested in what was *intended* to happen between two ex-spouses.
They are interested in what actually happens and how it is documented.

That may or may not align neatly with the decree.

Trap #4: Misinterpreting Separation Rules

A few times a year, someone asks me, "Would it help if we separated?"

I understand why people think that way.

Years ago, families tried to use separation as a strategy.

The schools caught on.

If you are "separated" but still living together, you generally must report combined income.

That means a separation must be genuine.

Separate households. Separate addresses. Separate financial realities.

If you are sharing a kitchen, a Netflix password, and a Costco membership, the school may be skeptical.

Trying to claim a separation that isn't genuine is a strategy that tends to backfire.

Trap #5: Assuming CSS Schools Follow FAFSA Rules

Just when you think you have a good FAFSA plan, the CSS Profile complicates matters.

As we have discussed throughout this book, the CSS Profile is a different animal.

That does not mean CSS schools are less generous. In many cases, it is the opposite.

It just means they want a fuller picture.

And one of the biggest differences lies in how they handle the non-custodial parent.

Non-Custodial Parents

This is often the most consequential difference between FAFSA schools and CSS schools.

More CSS schools require the non-custodial parent to complete separate financial forms—regardless of the family's emotional reality.

That can be very difficult.

And there is no use pretending otherwise.

Difficult Non-Custodial Parents

There is a non-custodial parent waiver process, often called an NCP waiver.

Schools usually categorize these situations into two groups:

- Refusal
- Legitimate exclusion

Refusal - Usually Denied

These situations are commonly denied:

"He refuses to fill it out."

This is very common and the most frequent reason waivers are denied.

"The divorce decree says he doesn't have to pay."
The school does not care what the family court ordered. That is not the rulebook they use.

"She refuses to help."
Unwillingness to pay is not the same as inability to pay.

"They haven't spoken in two years."
While terrible for the family, this often isn't enough for a waiver. Many colleges want to see **five to ten years or more of total absence** before they treat it as abandonment.

Legitimate Exclusion - More Likely Approved

These are the kinds of circumstances that may support a waiver:

- Documented abuse or domestic violence
- Restraining orders or protective orders
- Long-term abandonment with no contact and no support
- Incarceration
- Institutionalization
- Truly unknown whereabouts of the parent

It's important to note:

A waiver is almost never granted based only on the parent's or student's word.

Schools usually want third-party documentation from a counselor, therapist, clergy member, social worker, or another neutral professional.

Strategy: Get Help Early If the Other Parent Is Difficult

If the other parent is even somewhat cooperative, that's ideal.

If not, this is one of those areas where getting help can really make a difference.

I tell parents, "I am Switzerland."

While this situation is deeply personal and emotional for you, a professional in this field may be able to help your student more effectively by staying focused on the rules, documentation, and school strategy.

This book is here to help you do a lot on your own.

But I promised I would also tell you where seeking help may be wise.

This is definitely one of those places.

School Selection Still Matters

As with so many things in this book, school selection matters here, too.

If a school is FAFSA-only, the non-custodial parent may not matter much at all.

If a school requires the CSS Profile, the entire strategy may shift.

Some CSS schools are stricter than others. Some are more flexible. What works as a waiver argument at one school may fail at another.

So if you have a difficult non-custodial parent situation, that should absolutely be part of the school selection discussion.

Two CSS Stories

I want to give you a couple of examples so you don't walk away thinking that difficult CSS situations are hopeless.

Remarried Mom

I worked with a mom who had remarried a successful man.

The biological father was in and out of the picture.

At one point, he agreed to talk to me, and then he disappeared.

It would have been great to use his income on the FAFSA, but that was not realistic.

On top of that, the student had moderate academic scores, so school selection became critical.

We had to build a list that would not require the father's participation, would not overly penalize for the stepfather's financial picture, and would still fit the student academically.

There were both public and private schools that fit these parameters.

The student ultimately attended one of his preferred schools at a cost the family could manage.

Absent Mom

I had another student who had not had meaningful contact with her mother in years, though not long enough to easily qualify for an abandonment waiver.

I reached out to the mother, who was remarried and living in Europe.

She sent back a very rude email saying she had no intention of helping or disclosing anything, and that if the student wanted a free education, she could simply move to Europe.

Lovely.

Most of the schools on our list were CSS schools with strict requirements for both biological parents.

But one school—thankfully, also the student's top choice—really wanted her.

I presented that email along with an appeal, and the school granted a waiver.

She also received a generous award despite her father's income and assets.

So yes, there are hard cases.

But hard does not always mean hopeless.

Final Thoughts

There is no doubt that this is a challenging topic.

I have had parents tell me they waited until their youngest child went to college to finalize a divorce.

I have worked with others who have been divorced for years, only to find that college planning drags old emotions right back to the surface.

I have heard stories of abandonment and abuse.

I have also worked with divorced parents who joined every call together because they wanted to prioritize the student.

Every situation is different.

Every situation is complex.

But complex does not mean hopeless.

You should not assume the financial aid office views your family situation the way you do.

It does not. It sees rules, documentation, and formulas.

In many cases, divorced families have more financial aid potential than they realize.

But, as with virtually everything in this book, the sooner you start, the better.

Divorce is only one form of family complexity.

In today's world, many families are navigating remarriage, blended households, long-term partners, stepparents, and family structures that do not fit neatly into the boxes colleges prefer.

Unfortunately, the financial aid system has not evolved as quickly as families have.

Let's talk about that next.

30

Modern Families, Old Rules

If divorce complicates financial aid, blended families can turn that complication into a full-blown Rubik's Cube.

Financial aid rules were largely built around a traditional family model that often does not reflect modern reality.

To the financial aid office, the question is usually not:

"Who feels financially responsible for this child?"

It is:

"Who is in the household, and what resources are available?"

Those are not the same thing.

Modern families are complex. Financial aid forms are not.

That disconnect is where many of these issues begin.

Stepparent Income & Assets Count (Whether You Like It or Not)

This topic is one of the fastest ways to make a workshop go quiet.

One major reason is that college financial aid rules differ from family court rules.

In California and most other states I've worked with, family courts generally ignore income from a new spouse unless it is being used as imputed income.

The reasoning is simple: child support is the responsibility of the biological parents.

Colleges see it differently.

They are evaluating the household's ability to pay the cost of attendance, regardless of whether the income or assets belong to a biological parent.

Simply put:

All household income and assets are considered.

That can create an understandable emotional reaction.

"My new spouse shouldn't have to pay."
"I love them, but that is not my biological child—why do I have to pay?"
"We have a prenup."
"Our assets are completely separate."

I understand all of that.

But for the most part, schools focus less on where the money comes from and more on whether the household can contribute.

Another way to put it:

The FAFSA and CSS do not care whose child it is. They care whose household supports them.

Is There Anything We Can Do?

The primary way to address this is the same one I discussed in the last chapter: document that the other biological parent provides the majority of the student's support.

For example:

- Mom is remarried to a wealthy executive.
- Dad is single and earns $60,000.
- Even if the student lives with Mom, if Dad provides 51% of the student's actual support—say, by paying tuition, car costs, and health insurance—the FAFSA can use Dad.

That means the wealthy stepfather's income may be completely excluded from the federal calculation.

I am not encouraging anyone to fabricate information.

I am encouraging you to understand the rules and document reality accurately.

Some families also choose to delay remarriage until after the FAFSA is filed—or, in rare cases, until after college—if a new spouse's income would significantly reduce aid eligibility.

That is obviously a deeply personal decision and not one made solely for financial aid reasons. But it is a factor some families consider.

And yes, I have seen families make that choice.

Stepparent Example Story

Earlier in the book, I mentioned a family with a multimillion-dollar asset that they had not disclosed on our intake forms.

To be fair, this was a stepparent situation. They were not hiding it out of dishonesty.

The asset belonged to the stepfather, and a prenup was in place. They genuinely did not think it was relevant.

Imagine their shock when I explained that the financial aid office would not see it that way.

In their case, however, the biological father provided more support for the student than the biological mother, even though the son lived primarily with Mom and stepdad.

We documented the father's support.

As a result, even though the student applied exclusively to CSS schools, I was able to get those schools to remove the stepfather's assets from consideration, and the student received multiple generous offers.

Adoptions, Unmarried Partners, Same-Sex Relationships

I am grouping these together not because they are the same, but because they often share one central issue in the financial aid world:

Legal parenthood.

Legal Parenthood

In financial aid, biological parenthood does not always match legal parenthood.

You may adopt a child, making you a legal parent even if you are not the biological parent.

A child may be conceived with the help of a donor. If that donor is not on the birth certificate and has never had a formal parenting role, they may not be considered a legal parent.

Surrogacy can be even more complicated because state law matters. Some states, such as California, Nevada, and New York, have processes in which the surrogate may not appear on the birth certificate at all. Other states handle this differently.

That does not automatically make the surrogate a legal parent, but it illustrates how fact-specific these situations can be.

If you adopted the child or are the legal parent on paper, that usually matters far more than biology.

If you are unmarried, the determination often depends on whether your partner is on the birth certificate, whether they adopted the child, and sometimes whether they are part of the household.

As you can imagine, the combinations can become nearly endless.

As with many things in this book, CSS schools may dig deeper than FAFSA schools. But both are looking for legal parenthood, not just a biological connection.

Here is a simple chart that may help:

Person	Included on FAFSA?	Included on CSS?
Parent on birth certificate	Yes	Yes
Legal adoptive parent	Yes	Yes
Biological parent NOT on birth certificate	No	Maybe
Ex-partner (never married, never adopted)	No	No
Current stepparent	Yes (If married to FAFSA parent)	Yes

In financial aid, legal parenthood often matters more than biological relationships alone.

This is not an exhaustive list of every possible family structure, but it gives you a sense of how schools often distinguish between biological and legal parenthood.

If your situation is complex and that distinction feels murky, this is another area where getting help may be wise.

Checking the wrong box—or failing to explain your story correctly—can cost you thousands.

Modern Family Example

Here is a real-life example of how biological relationships and legal parenthood do not always match.

I met with a woman who had been in a long-term same-sex relationship.

Due to the era in which their relationship took place, they were unable to legally marry.

They decided to have a child.

She asked a close friend to be the donor. She gave birth to the child, and she and her partner raised the child together for several years.

They later broke up, and many years later, the child was now getting ready for college.

When we first met, her main question was:

How will the financial aid system view this situation?

Would the donor—who was technically the biological father—need to provide financial information even though he had never acted as a parent?

Would her former partner, whom she had not seen in over a decade, need to complete the CSS?

It all came down to legal parenthood.

My client was the only person on the birth certificate, and her former partner had never legally adopted the child.

That mattered.

If the partner had been on the birth certificate or had legally adopted the child, the analysis would have changed.

If the donor had been on the birth certificate but had never provided any support, we likely would have pursued a waiver.

But if he had ever held the child out as his own or provided support, that could have changed the analysis, too.

Wild, right?

These scenarios are part of modern family life. If your situation is complicated—even if it does not look exactly like this one—you can probably see why I recommend getting some help when biology, legal parenthood, and household reality do not line up neatly.

Multiple Household & Shared Expense Situations

Financial aid forms, like everything else, are meant to fit into a neat little box.

When has life ever worked that way?

It is not possible to detail every possible scenario.

But a few principles apply consistently.

Two situations often arise:

Your student spends time in multiple households.
Or, other people in the home may be sharing expenses.

The first big principle is this:
Do not assume. Do not guess.

Those assumptions can be costly.

It is easy to assume that the student should use the parent they spend the most time with or the parent who writes the largest check each month.

But I regularly see cases where the lower-income parent provides more overall support.

One parent may write a large child support check, while the other covers everything else.

The second principle is this:
Documentation matters.

If your student is moving between multiple homes, or if there are other people in the household contributing to expenses—such as an adult sibling or other relative—document who is paying what.

The FAFSA is not likely to ask much about these kinds of arrangements. CSS schools, however, may dig deeper.

I have even heard of schools noticing multiple tax returns tied to the same address and asking follow-up questions as a result.

Documentation helps.

Final Thoughts

The topics covered in this chapter reflect modern realities.

These scenarios are also situations that schools often cannot fully understand just by looking at your tax return and the aid forms.

The good news is that, for the most part, schools understand that life gets messy.

They know not every family fits a 1950s definition of the American household.

But they will not know your situation unless you explain it.

And the response will vary by school, which is another reason school selection remains an important consideration for financial aid.

So, do not make assumptions about how your family should be presented.

Review the facts. Understand the rules. Document accordingly.

Messy family structures are common. They do not make planning impossible.

But you do need to understand the rules before they are applied to you.

Family structure is one source of complexity.

But even if your household is straightforward, life can still throw financial curveballs:

job loss, disability, business downturns, medical crises, retirement, and caring for aging parents.

And when those things happen, the numbers on your tax return may no longer reflect reality.

In the next chapter, we'll cover what to do when life changes faster than financial aid formulas can keep up.

31

When the Numbers Don't Reflect Reality

As we've discussed throughout this book, timing plays a major role in financial aid.

And sometimes, timing creates a problem.

Financial aid formulas rely on a snapshot in time—often based on tax returns from two years ago.

But life does not always cooperate with that timeline.

Your income may have dropped.
Your expenses may have increased.
Or that tax return may reflect a one-time event that will never happen again.

In this chapter, we're not going to dive into the mechanics of appeals—that's coming next.

Instead, we'll focus on situations where the numbers don't tell the full story.

So if one of these applies to you, know two things:

You're not alone.

And you may have options.

Professional Review

A Professional Review (also called Professional Judgment) is the process of telling a college:

"The numbers on our financial aid forms do not reflect our actual ability to pay."

Financial aid administrators have the authority—granted under federal law—to adjust your financial aid data.

But they are not required to.

And as you might expect, some schools are more flexible than others.

Many families don't even know this process exists.

This means they often accept an initial offer as final, even though it may not be.

The reality is, **the formula is often the starting point—not the final verdict.**

Most professional reviews fall into a handful of common categories.

Let's start with the one schools probably see most often:

Income Went Down Year Over Year

This is a scenario I see regularly.

What appears on a tax return from two years ago may not reflect what is happening today.

It could be due to a job loss, a role change, or a disability.

I've also seen many situations where someone leaves a corporate job to start a business.

Most businesses don't generate significant income in the first few years.

Side note: Remember when I mentioned starting a business earlier in the book?
This is one of those situations where timing can create a meaningful difference in reported income.

For those experiencing a downturn in an existing business, we'll address that shortly.

There are also more serious life events that can impact income.

One of the most difficult—and unfortunately, not uncommon—is the loss of a parent.

We've had families go through this during the college process.

I don't bring this up lightly.

But if it were to happen in your family, I want you to know there is a process to address it.

A significant change like this can—and should—be brought to the attention of the financial aid office.

Regardless of the reason, the challenge is the same:

The FAFSA or CSS may not reflect your current reality.

How Schools Typically Handle This

The good news is that this is a common scenario—and schools are accustomed to it.

Most financial aid offices have a defined process for reviewing changes in income.

Your first step is simple:
Call the financial aid office and explain your situation.
They will tell you exactly what documentation they want to see.

Typically, this includes:

- Updated tax returns
- Pay stubs
- Termination notices
- Physician documentation
- Business financials
- Death certificate

They will often ask you to estimate:

- Your current year's income
- And sometimes the following year's income

Which leads to the obvious question:

"How am I supposed to know that?"

You don't.

But they are looking for a reasonable, good-faith estimate based on what you know today.

The important thing to understand is that schools generally do not expect families to absorb a major life change in silence.

An Unexpected Increase in Income

Not all income changes are negative.

Sometimes they are quite positive.

However, if that increase is a one-time event, you don't want it to distort your financial aid picture.

Common causes include:

- One-time bonus
- Commission spike
- Profit-sharing event
- Stock vesting / RSU payout
- Severance package

- Roth conversion
- Capital gains event
- Inheritance-related taxable event

These are typically non-recurring.

In some cases, you may even report income that you never actually received.

This is often referred to as phantom income.

All of these situations may need to be explained to the school.

A strong year does not necessarily mean a sustainable ability to pay.

Schools understand that—when it's clearly explained and properly documented.

Major Expenses the Formula Doesn't See

This deserves its own section because it can significantly impact financial aid.

Whether you are caring for an aging parent, supporting a disabled family member, managing your own health, or dealing with catastrophic home repairs, these are real financial burdens.

And they often don't appear on the FAFSA or the CSS Profile.

Let's look at a few of these more closely.

Care for Others and Major Medical Experiences

Situations like caring for an aging parent, a disabled sibling, or a family member with a serious illness can significantly affect your financial picture.

In one case, a family was initially denied financial aid based on income and assets.

But their situation changed when an elderly parent moved in and required care.

They were suddenly spending over $10,000 per month.

We requested a professional review, provided documentation, and the school issued a more favorable package.

These situations don't require the person to live in your home.

I've worked with families paying $12,000–$15,000 per month for assisted living.

This had a meaningful impact once properly documented.

This can also include long-term therapy or psychiatric care.

While these expenses are unfortunately common today, they are still worth highlighting.

Catastrophic Home Repairs

Some major expenses are personal.

Others are catastrophic.

Unfortunately, events like natural disasters can create financial situations that the formulas were never designed to handle.

I live in Los Angeles, and you may recall the fires in Malibu and Altadena.

I worked on several of these situations during that time period.

People lost homes—in many cases, everything.

I worked with one family who lost their home and business in that fire.

Unfortunately, due to the high concentration of loss, some desirable local schools, such as Pepperdine, LMU, and USC, had limited ability to help.

We were able to secure some additional funding, but not as much as we would have hoped.

This is why I remind people that there is no guarantee you'll get an increased award.

I helped another family who wasn't impacted by the fire but by a hillside collapse that destroyed homes right below them.

We had already completed all applications and had offers pending when this happened.

For safety, the city shut off power, gas, and water to the area.

Their home went from a multimillion-dollar valuation to nearly zero overnight.

The mother was well compensated—but can you imagine the financial pressure they were under?

The good news?

We submitted an appeal with extensive documentation, and the school reevaluated the situation.

By now, you're probably noticing a theme:

Clear communication—and strong documentation—matter.

Business Fluctuations & Phantom Income

As someone who has owned multiple businesses since leaving college, I've seen firsthand how dramatically income can fluctuate from year to year.

Market conditions.
Economic shifts.
Regulatory changes.
Business reinvestment.

All of these can impact reported income.

But there's another issue that can be even more confusing:

Phantom income.

Phantom Income

I briefly mentioned phantom income before, but it's worth exploring further because it can be problematic.

Phantom income is taxable income that is "passed through" to a business owner's personal tax return, even though they did not receive a cash distribution from the business.

I see this happen in a few scenarios:

Business reinvestment:
A K-1 shows $100,000 in profit, but the funds were reinvested into the business.

Debt forgiveness:
A forgiven loan is treated as taxable income.

Minority ownership:
A parent owns 10% of a business that reports profits but receives no distribution.

The last scenario is common and can adversely affect financial aid.

I've seen significant K-1 impacts, even for parents with modest incomes.

For business owners, a professional review is often necessary.

We know that our situation rarely fits into a simple box.

Whether we are applying for a mortgage or filing taxes, very few things are completely straightforward.

The good news?

The schools understand how a business works, and if there is proper documentation, your reconsideration may be successful.

The bad news?

The schools understand how a business works.

What do I mean?

They are adept at identifying attempts to mislead them.

Not Every Problem Is a Life Event

It's also important to understand that errors happen.

More often than you might expect.

The school can make a mistake.
Your CPA can make a mistake.
Even a W-2 or 1099 can be reported incorrectly.

The key is not to assume every number is interpreted correctly.

Let me share a couple of stories about this.

Rollover Trouble

A year or so ago, I worked with someone who retired from a long career with the sheriff's department.

As part of her retirement, a portion of her pension was disbursed, and she rolled it into another retirement account.

A rollover like this is not a taxable event.

It is, however, recorded on the tax return as a rollover event.

The school added this to the family's income, and since it was in the mid-six figures, it ruled them out for financial aid.

Is it an error?

You could probably argue either way, but in most cases, the schools understand the situation, and it doesn't negatively affect financial aid.

However, this has happened a couple of times over the years, and we've had to appeal.

Successfully, I might add, but the point is that we had to go through the extra work.

Don't assume the financial aid office will get it right every time.

Here's another example.

Double-Counted Asset

I told the story of the mom who lived in Europe and was uncooperative; we obtained a waiver to exclude her income.

Well, the story didn't end there.

After the waiver, the offer was lower than we expected.

So I spoke with Dad and the financial aid office.

After some back and forth, the financial aid officer said, "Oh my goodness, we counted an asset twice."

The result?

The final offer was substantially more than we expected.

Again, don't assume everyone has the right information.

When the Numbers Don't Match Reality: Final Thoughts

Financial aid formulas are designed to create consistency.

But no formula can fully capture every family's situation.

When your numbers don't tell the whole story, you may have the opportunity to explain the difference.

Whether it's:

- A drop in income

- A one-time spike
- Significant expenses
- Business complexity
- Or simply an error

...these situations often require a closer look.

For many families, simply knowing that a review is possible helps alleviate the stress of an initial offer that feels incorrect.

There are no guarantees.

Schools are not required to make adjustments.

But families who are prepared—those who document clearly and communicate effectively—give themselves the best chance at a better outcome.

And that brings us to the next phase of this process.

At some point, however, all of this planning, positioning, and preparation turns into something tangible:

An award letter.

And for many families, that's where the confusion really begins.

The numbers don't always make sense.
The language can be misleading.
And what looks like a "good" award often isn't.

In the next section, we will walk through what those offers actually mean—how to evaluate, compare, and, when appropriate, challenge them.

Getting the offer is not the finish line.

It's where the real decisions begin.

PART VII

After the Award: Where the Real Decisions Happen

You're back at the kitchen table where we started this discussion.

Her laptop is open as the emails from her top schools have finally arrived.

The award letter is ready.

You gather around the screen.

She opens the portal.

After everything:

The planning, research, and applications…

This is the moment.

You click the link, read the offer, and…

At this point, it's important to remember something:

This is not quite the end of the process.

But it is also not automatically the beginning of a negotiation.

For many families, the **work done earlier in this book**—understanding the system, planning ahead, choosing schools carefully, and positioning finances thoughtfully—**is exactly what helps produce a fair result.**

Often, the offer reflects that preparation.

That is the goal.

Still, this stage matters.

Because what a family expects and what they receive are not always the same.

Sometimes the numbers do not reflect reality.
Sometimes circumstances changed after the FAFSA year.
Sometimes income shifted.
A business slowed.
Medical expenses appeared.
A parent lost a job.
Or there were factors that the original application simply could not capture.
And sometimes, a school just needs more context.

This isn't only about dollars.

It is also about understanding.

The language can feel optimistic — but vague.

The numbers may not quite make sense.

And you may still be asking:

"Is this actually a good offer?"

That is where this section comes in.

Up to this point, much of what we discussed focused on preparation:

- Understanding how the system works
- Positioning finances thoughtfully
- Choosing schools strategically

- Aligning your student's direction

Now the focus shifts.

Evaluation.
Comparison.
And, when appropriate, advocacy.

Not every family will need an appeal.

But some families will face situations where additional review, clarification, or planning can still make an important difference.

And those are the moments we want you prepared for.

In this section, we're going to walk through:

- How to read and understand an offer letter
- How to compare offers effectively
- How to recognize when something deserves another look
- And when — and how — to ask for more information or reconsideration

Your student already did the hard work to earn admission.

Now we make sure the path forward still makes sense for your family.

The award letter is not always the finish line.
Sometimes it is confirmation.
Sometimes it is a conversation.
And occasionally…
It is the beginning of a strategy.

32

Understanding the Award Letter

I've never measured a parent's heart rate when an award letter arrives…

…but I'd bet it's high.

As I mentioned earlier, a big part of that reaction comes from one assumption:

This is it. This is what we are getting.

Sometimes it is.

Sometimes it isn't.

And before you think about appeals, negotiations, or next steps, the first job is simply understanding what you are looking at.

I coach families not to overreact to the first number they see.

The goal at this stage is not immediate action.

It is clarity.

Because you cannot decide whether an offer is good, disappointing, incomplete, or worth revisiting until you understand how it is constructed.

That starts here.

A Misleading Title

"Award letter."

Sounds great, doesn't it?

Like you won something.

And sometimes you did.

But the name can also create confusion.

Let's start with what an award letter is **not**.

An award letter is not:

- A bill
- A final four-year cost projection
- Automatically the best offer a school can provide
- Proof that something went wrong

It is something else entirely.

It is the school's proposed way of helping cover the Cost of Attendance using the resources available to them.

That may include:

Grants
Scholarships
Work-study
Loans
And family contribution expectations

The important thing is understanding how those pieces fit together.

Because not every dollar shown on an award letter lowers your cost in the same way.

A better comparison?

It's a little like looking at a new car.

You see the sticker.

You see the features.

You see the suggested price.

But before deciding whether it is a good deal, you usually ask:

"What is actually included?"

"What do I really need?"

"And what will this cost me in practice?"

Award letters work much the same way.

The goal is not to react to the first number.

It is to understand the story the offer is telling.

Once we understand that story, we can decide whether anything needs another look.

The Illusion of Aid

This is where families get tripped up.

They see a large "Total Aid" number at the bottom and think:

"Wow, we got a great deal."

But that number is often misleading.

Here's a simple example:

Total Aid: $50,500

Sounds strong.

Until you break it down:

- $20,000 — School grant
- $5,000 — Work-study
- $5,500 — Student loan

- $20,000 — Parent PLUS loan

Only one of those reduces your cost:

The $20,000 grant.

The rest?

- Loans must be repaid.
- Work-study must be earned.

So while the letter says $50,500…

Your real reduction is $20,000.

That's a big difference.

And it completely changes the picture of that "award."

The best way to understand the award letter is to break it down into its fundamental parts.

The Five Elements of the Award Letter

Once you understand the structure, the confusion starts to fade.

Reduced confusion leads to better analysis.

Solid analysis is the first step to a strong appeal.

Cost of Attendance

The school's estimate of what one year will cost.

This includes both fixed and estimated expenses (we'll break that down next).

Student Aid Index

Your FAFSA-derived number.

This does not change from school to school.

If the CSS Profile is used, the school may adjust this internally.

Gift Aid

This is the money you don't repay.

Includes:

- Federal grants (Pell)
- State grants (Cal Grant, TAP, TEXAS Grant, HOPE, etc.)
- Institutional grants and scholarships

This is what actually reduces your cost.

Borrowed Money

Loans.

Includes:

- Federal student loans
- Parent PLUS loans

If it has to be repaid:

It is not aid; it is financing.

Other Self-Help Aid

Options—not discounts.

Includes:

- Work-study
- Payment plans

Work-study can be valuable, and I typically recommend it.

But it still requires work to earn the money.

Cost of Attendance Breakdown

Not all parts of COA are equal.

Direct Costs (More Fixed)

Tuition
Fees
Room & board

These are generally accurate.

Estimated Costs (Flexible)

Books
Travel
Personal expenses

These vary widely.

For example:

If your student lives close to home:

Travel might be minimal, and they can come home to do laundry.

If they're across the country:

Travel and personal expenses might be significantly higher.

This is where families often think, "Oh, thank goodness…"

…and then look closer.

Net Price vs. True Out-of-Pocket Cost

Most families instinctively think:

COA – Total Aid = What we pay

But that includes loans.

So it's not the real number.

Here's what actually matters:

Net Price

COA – Gift Aid

This is your starting point.

True Out-of-Pocket

Net Price + Borrowing

This is your real financial burden.

Your Simple Goal

When you look at an award letter, you are trying to answer three questions:

1. **How much is free?**
2. **How much is borrowed?**
3. **What is our real out-of-pocket cost?**

That's it.

Everything else is noise.

Understanding how to break down the award letter is the first step in reducing the stress that comes with seeing those numbers for the first time.

But once you have multiple offers in front of you…

A new problem arises.

They all look different.

Different formats, terminology, and structures.

So how do you actually compare them?

That's where we're going next.

33

Comparing Offers the Right Way

"I have no idea who is offering what."

I hear that all the time.

And honestly?

That's not your fault.

Award letters are not designed to be easily compared.

Different formats.

Different terminology.

Different structures.

But one thing is consistent:

Every school is trying to make its offer look the most competitive.

"Why Do They Make It So Complicated?"

"I feel like they're trying to trick me."

I wouldn't go that far…

But I understand why it feels that way.

Earlier in the book, I asked you to think of schools as businesses.

And like any business, they are trying to attract customers (students) to buy their product (a degree).

So when they present an offer, they are doing what any business would do:

Putting themselves in the best possible light.

At this stage, they are trying to "win" your student's enrollment.

And they know that one of the biggest drivers of decision-making for families is cost.

So it helps to reframe the award letter as what it really is:

Part financial document. Part marketing piece.

Behind the scenes, schools are also managing something called yield.

Without getting too deep into it, here's the simple version:

Schools aren't just trying to admit students.

They're trying to enroll the right number of students… at the right price.

Your job is to look past the presentation—and evaluate what's actually best for your family.

The Award Letter:
Part financial document.
Part marketing piece.

Creating Uniformity

You're trying to compare apples to apples…

But schools are handing you apples, oranges—and a few things that look like fruit but aren't.

There have been attempts to standardize award letters.

So far, none have been successful.

So until that happens, you need your own system.

Here's a simple way to categorize what you're seeing:

Item on Award	Sounds Like	Actually Is	Rating	What to Know
Grants	"Free money"	Money you don't repay (free money)	Great	Reduces Your Cost
Scholarships	Earned awards	Merit/outside money (free money)	Great	Check renewal terms
Work-study	"Aid"	Job opportunity	Neutral	Must be earned
Student Loans	"Student aid"	Debt	Caution	Limited, but still debt
Parent Loans	"Parent option"	Debt in the parent's name	High Caution	Easy to overuse
Private Loans	"Gap help"	Bank loan	Be highly cautious	Least flexible, highest risk

Not everything labeled as "aid" actually lowers your cost.

If it has to be paid back, it's not aid.

It's a payment plan.

The Big "Aid" Mistake

This is where families often feel the most misled.

The most common mistake?

Comparing the "Total Aid" number.

Let's walk through an example.

Both schools:

- Cost of Attendance: $90,000
- SAI: $20,000

School A:

- "Aid": $60,000

School B:

- "Aid": $45,000

Most families look at that and say:

"School A is clearly the better deal."

And honestly, that's exactly what the school hopes you'll conclude.

But here's the part the headline number hides:

School A includes $25,000 in loans
School B includes $5,000 in loans

Let's break it down properly:

	School A	School B
COA	$90,000	$90,000
"Total Aid"	$60,000	$45,000
Gift Aid	$35,000	$40,000
Loans Included	$25,000	$5,000
Net Price	**$55,000**	**$50,000**
Family Cash	$30,000	$45,000
Debt Taken On	$25,000	$5,000

The offer with the biggest "aid" number is not always the one that costs your family the least in the long run.

What This Means

School A looks better.

But $25,000 of that "aid" is debt.

So the real comparison is:

- **School A:** $55,000 cost, $25,000 borrowed
- **School B:** $50,000 cost, $5,000 borrowed

School B is cheaper overall.

School A requires less cash today.

And that's the nuance.

There isn't always a single "right" answer.

But there is a **clearer picture.**

The Impact of Interest

There's one more piece missing from every award letter:

Interest.

Loans don't just delay payment—they increase it.

That $25,000 in loans at School A?

That could become $30,000… $35,000… or more over time.

The $5,000 at School B?

Closer to $6,000 or $7,000.

Same degree.

Same starting point.

Very different long-term cost.

The Four-Year Question

Most families, and frankly, even professionals, focus primarily on the first year.

But that can be a costly mistake.

Remember one of our earlier questions:

"How long does it actually take to graduate?"

Now factor that into your thinking:

- Is this aid guaranteed for all four years?
- Do you have to requalify each year?
- Could your income change?
- Will the school adjust aid over time?

You're not committing to one year.

You're committing to a full journey.

Year one matters.

But you're making a four-year decision.

It's a lot to consider.

And these decisions have huge implications for you and your student.

This can add a lot of stress.

To help ease some of that stress, let's discuss a process to compare offers.

This may not make them apples to apples, but at least it won't be apples and rutabagas.

"How Do I Compare?"

When you strip away the noise, you're really answering four questions:

What is the real net price?
How much is free vs. borrowed?
Will this hold for four years?
What happens if life changes?

If you like spreadsheets, build one.

If you don't, grab a legal pad and write it out by hand.

The format matters far less than the process.

Once you distill the offers into the same core categories, the decision usually becomes much clearer.

The goal is clarity,
not head-scratching.

Here is a simple example of what a side-by-side comparison might look like:

	School A	School B	School C
Cost of Attendance	$90,000	$82,000	$76,000
Gift Aid	$35,000	$40,000	$28,000
Student Loans	$5,500	$5,500	$5,500
Parent Loans	$20,000	$5,000	$0
Work Study	$3,000	$2,500	$0
Net Price	$55,000	$42,000	$48,000
Total Borrowing	$25,500	$10,500	$5,500
Estimated Family Cash Flow	$29,500	$31,500	$42,500
Guaranteed 4 Years?	Partial	Yes	Merit Only
CSS or FAFSA?	CSS	FAFSA	CSS
Graduation Rate	78%	92%	64%
Avg. Time to Degree	4.5 years	4 years	5 years
Emotional Notes	"Dream school"	"Loved campus"	"Too far away?"

A simple side-by-side comparison can quickly reveal differences that award letters often hide.

Notice what happened here:

The school with the highest "aid" number was not automatically the best financial decision.
And the school with the lowest first-year cost may not stay that way over four years.

This is why creating a side-by-side comparison matters.

Because once the emotion of the award letter wears off, you still have to live with the financial reality of the decision.

The Emotional Tradeoff

Now let's be honest.

This isn't just a math problem.

There's emotion involved:

prestige,
dream schools,

peer pressure ("Everyone is going there…" "I'll be miserable if I don't go…")

This emotion should also factor into the decision.

But here's the caution:

It's easy to justify a higher price when a school feels like the "right" one.

Just make sure you understand what that decision actually costs over the long term.

We will explore that a little bit more in the final section of this book.

What's Next?

I keep emphasizing that the award letter is not automatically the end of the process.

But it is also not necessarily the beginning of an appeal.

So far, you've:

- Broken down the offers
- Compared them properly
- Looked past the "total aid" number
- Thought through the trade-offs

That work matters.

Because **many families discover that the original offer was fair once they understand how it was calculated.**

Others uncover gaps.

Changed circumstances.

Missing context.

Or situations where the numbers no longer reflect reality.

And those are the moments when another conversation may make sense.

Not every family will need another conversation.

But some families should absolutely have one.

The key is knowing the difference.

That's where we're headed next.

34

Appeals & Negotiation

I come from a Sicilian family.

Negotiation isn't just a tactic in my family.

It's practically a cultural tradition.

"What's the cash price?" wasn't merely a line from a TV show growing up.

I was raised to ask questions.

To understand the numbers.

To look for options.

And yes… sometimes to negotiate.

But experience has also taught me something important:

Not every situation should turn into a negotiation.

Sometimes the original offer is fair.

Sometimes the planning done years earlier worked exactly as intended.

And sometimes the best decision is simply recognizing that you already have a good outcome.

Other times?

The numbers do not reflect reality.

Income changed.
A business slowed.
Medical expenses arose.
Circumstances shifted.
Or information that matters never made it into the original application.

Those are different situations.

And those are often the moments when another conversation may be appropriate.

I've seen the look on parents' faces when the award letter arrives.

You're tired.

You've been through months — sometimes years — of planning.

When that number appears, it can feel like:

"Well… I guess this is what it is."

Sometimes it is.

Sometimes it isn't.

The key is understanding the difference.

Because this is the point where many families stop.

And occasionally…

It is also where an important opportunity still exists.

What An Appeal Really Is

Most parents say:

"We need to ask them for more money."

That's the wrong starting point.

An appeal is not simply a request for more money—

even if that ends up being the result.

It's a clarification.

A clear explanation of why the school's current assessment of your financial situation is inaccurate.

That shift in mindset changes everything.

Professional Judgment (The Formal Process)

You've heard me mention this before.

This is the official name for the appeal process.

It happens after the initial offer and gives you the opportunity to present:

- New information
- Clarifying information
- Additional context

Because here's the truth:

Financial aid forms are designed to fit your life into a tidy box.

Life doesn't work that way.

The FAFSA provides no room to explain.

The CSS offers only a small box.

An appeal is where the real story gets told.

Where to Appeal

This varies by school.

Some require a portal.
Some use a web form.
Others allow direct email.
Occasionally, you'll work directly with an advisor.

Before you do anything:

Check the school's financial aid website and follow their process exactly.

Schools are usually very specific about how they want appeals submitted.

Don't improvise here.

When You Should Appeal

When I sit down with families, this is often where the conversation shifts.

Up until now, much of our focus has been on planning.

Now we're looking at something real.

The offers have arrived.

The numbers are on the table.

And the question becomes:

"Does this deserve another look?"

Sometimes the answer is no.

The planning worked.

The offer is fair.

And the next step is simply moving forward with confidence.

Other times, the answer is yes.

The key is understanding the difference.

Here are some of the most common situations where an appeal, reconsideration, or additional conversation may make sense.

1. Income That Doesn't Reflect Reality

The FAFSA uses income from two years ago.

A lot can change.

Examples:

- Job loss
- Reduced income
- One-time bonus or RSU event
- Severance
- Misinterpreted income

The key is clarity.

For example:

"This was a non-taxable rollover and does not reflect available income."

"This income was a one-time event and is not expected to continue."

2. Business Income Is Misunderstood

Business owners see this all the time.

Examples:

- K-1 "phantom income."
- Retained earnings
- Gross revenue mistaken for actual take-home income

Simple clarification works:

"Income reported was retained in the business and not available for personal use."

"This figure reflects gross revenue, not net income after expenses."

3. Asset Misinterpretation

Assets are one of the biggest sources of confusion.

Examples:

- Overstated home value
- Illiquid assets
- Restricted assets (like prenups or irrevocable trusts)

Sometimes, it's just about adding context.

I had a client who inherited a home that appeared valuable on paper but was incredibly difficult to sell.

When he spoke to the financial aid office, he jokingly said:

"You're welcome to take the house if you can sell it."

I don't recommend that approach…

But we followed up with actual comps and a clear explanation of the property.

The school adjusted the valuation.

Same asset.

Better understood.

4. Expenses the Formula Doesn't See

This is a big one.

The formulas don't capture real-life obligations like:

- Elder care
- Medical expenses
- Long-term care
- Therapy or specialized support

These can be substantial.

And the school won't know unless you tell them.

"We are currently responsible for significant ongoing care expenses not reflected in our tax return."

5. Mistakes (They Happen More Than You Think)

Sometimes, the data is simply wrong.

- Data entry errors
- Misinterpretation
- Double-counted assets

I've seen a school assume a family had $25,000/month in discretionary spending.

Reality?

$2,500.

The rest was pass-through money for elder care.

That's not a small difference—it's everything.

6. Offer Doesn't Match Expectations

If you've done your homework:

- Net Price Calculator
- Research on aid policies
- Comparable schools

Sometimes, the data is simply wrong.

That's a valid reason to ask questions.

Sometimes that leads to a correction.

Sometimes it reveals that the school simply isn't as flexible as you hoped.

When NOT to Appeal

Now let me give you the other side of this — because it is equally important.

Not every situation calls for an appeal.

And sometimes, the best decision is to leave things exactly as they are.

You may not need an appeal if:

- Nothing has changed
- The information submitted was accurate
- The offer reflects what the school would reasonably be expected to provide
- The planning already produced a strong result

Sometimes families do everything right.

And the outcome reflects that.

That is not a failure.

That is the goal.

When the Answer Is "*This Is a Good Outcome*"

Sometimes a strong offer comes in…

And the instinct becomes:

"Should we ask for more anyway?"

I had a client in exactly that situation.

He received a very generous offer, but his income had shifted and he wondered whether an appeal still made sense.

On the surface, it sounded reasonable.

But we also knew something else:

His tax return included aggressive write-offs that were already working in his favor.

Requesting additional review could have invited a deeper evaluation —

And potentially a less favorable outcome.

We advised him not to appeal.

That was not the answer he expected.

But it was the right one.

Because this process is not only about improving an offer.

It is also about protecting a good result.

Appeals are a tool.

Not every situation needs one.

And sometimes the smartest strategy is recognizing when the work you already did succeeded.

You Don't Have Documentation

This part is simple—and important:

If you can't prove it, don't say it.

Schools rely on:

- Tax documents
- Statements
- Letters
- Verifiable data

Your job is to:

- Be organized
- Highlight key points
- Make it easy for them to understand the situation.

What To Say

If you're like most parents, this is probably the part that makes you the most uncomfortable.

What do I actually say?

How do I say it without sounding demanding… or desperate… or like I don't know what I'm doing?

The good news is—you don't need to be perfect.

You just need to be clear and calm.

We Were Hoping for More

Instead of:

"This isn't enough. We need more money."

Say this:

We would like to understand the reasons for this decision and provide any supplementary information to ensure your office has a complete view of our situation.

Another School Gave More

Instead of:

"Another school gave us more."

Say this:

We have received a different financial picture from a comparable institution, and we hope to understand whether there is additional flexibility available here.

I Don't Think We Can Afford This

Instead of:

"We can't afford this."

Say this:

Given our current circumstances, this financial situation is challenging for our family. Could you help us understand the process for requesting a professional review to ensure our most recent information is reflected?

A Mistake

Instead of:

"You made a mistake."

Say this:

We want to ensure that our financial information was interpreted as intended—would it be helpful if we provided additional context for a few of these details?

Important Reminder

While it may feel like it, this is not a win-or-lose situation.

This is not an argument.

You are very unlikely to argue your way to a better outcome.

The goal of the appeal is to start a conversation where clarification, understanding, and updates are possible.

A Step-by-Step Appeals Strategy

We've covered a lot in this chapter, so I just want to provide the step-by-step process that I use for appeals.

Call First

Start with a conversation. Avoid keeping everything digital.

I'm going to pause here for a moment because this is where I see a lot of families hesitate.

Not because they don't know what to do...
But because they're uncomfortable doing it.

Some of the biggest breakthroughs happen on a phone call.

Yes, email works.

Yes, portals work.

But conversations move things forward.

I can't tell you how many times we've gone back and forth through email or a portal and gotten nowhere.

Then we pick up the phone—and everything changes.

Within a few minutes, someone pulls up the file, looks at it with fresh eyes, and says something like:

"Oh... I see what's going on here."

And just like that, we have clarity—and a path forward.

It's not that the school was hiding anything.

A real conversation can cut through confusion much faster than a long email chain.

Follow Their Process

Don’t go rogue.

Schools are typically very clear about how they want the appeal to work. Don't try to go your own way or assume you'll have a better chance by not following their process.

Provide Documentation

Organized. Clear. Highlighted.

Focus on making their job easier, rather than just throwing them a bunch of documents and hoping they figure it out.

Be Clear and Concise

Facts are better than emotion.

I know that it is easier said than done.

However, keeping emotion out of your appeal is critical.

Anything other than facts might hurt more than help.

Follow-Up

Be polite. Be consistent.

If you do it correctly, they will appreciate your persistence.

Be Persistent

Opportunities can arise late in the process. Don't give up.

This is one of the most overlooked strategies.

Financial aid isn’t static.

As students commit elsewhere:

Spots open
Money gets reallocated
Budgets shift

We've seen successful appeals happen:

Weeks later
Months later
Even right before school starts

We had a family who submitted an appeal and didn't see much progress initially.

It would have been easy to assume that was the final answer.

Instead, they stayed in touch—politely and consistently.

A couple of months later, they reached out again.

At that point, some students had declined offers, and funds had opened up.

The result?

A revised offer that was significantly better than the original.

Same student. Same situation.

Different timing.

Don't become a nuisance.

But don't disappear either.

Take a Breath

I want you to take a breath here.

Because this part of the process can feel overwhelming.

You've done everything you were supposed to do.

You helped your student.

You filled out the forms.
You waited.

And now you're being asked to go back and question the result.

That can feel uncomfortable.

But it is sometimes an important part of the process.

The families who tend to do best in this phase are not always the loudest.

They are usually the most organized, the most prepared, and the most persistent.

Because in many cases, financial aid is not just about qualifying.

It is about advocating clearly for your family's reality.

And sometimes, that advocacy can dramatically change the outcome.

35

Using Student Loans Strategically

Loans and debt of any kind are a hotly debated topic.

On one side, you have voices like Dave Ramsey who say you should avoid debt entirely.

On the other hand, you have advisors to the very wealthy who use debt strategically—what they call leverage.

So who's right?

The real answer is:
They both are.

Debt without a plan can be incredibly destructive.

When used strategically, debt can be a powerful tool.

Student loans are no different.

Without a plan, they can become incredibly harmful.

Used strategically, they can become a tool that protects your broader financial future.

That's how I want you to think about them throughout this chapter.

I don't specialize in student loans.

When choosing specific loan products or repayment structures, I rely on professionals who specialize in that area.

However, I discuss loan strategies in general with most of my clients.

The Three Ways to Pay

If you recall, we talked about the three primary ways to pay for college:

Out of income (today's money)
Out of assets (tomorrow's money - including retirement)
Borrow (future assets and income)

Many families I speak with are okay with the first two but are dead set against loans.

That is understandable.

According to USDebtClock.org, the average student debt per person in the United States is about four times that of credit card debt.

That concerns people.

What is even worse is that, according to USA Today, senior citizens owe $125 billion in student debt, and over 1 million have their Social Security garnished to repay it.

At this point, most parents are probably thinking:

"Ivana… why would we ever consider loans then?"

While those numbers look scary — and they are — to me, that represents loans without a plan.

Going back to our three ways to pay, the goal isn't to eliminate any of them.

The goal is to find the right mix for your situation.

The reality is that borrowing isn't the enemy…
Borrowing without a plan is.

The Biggest Student Loan Mistake

"I've drained my savings, borrowed from my 401(k), and now I probably have to take out a loan. Is there anything I can do?"

That's how a call with a father began a few months ago.

And it highlights the biggest mistake families make with student loans:

They only consider them when they are out of options.

By that point, the damage is often already done.

Each of the three ways to pay for college has potential drawbacks.

Let's be honest: college is an enormous expense, no matter how you frame it.

We will work to lower that cost as much as possible, but in the end, the system is designed so that you will have a portion of the cost left to cover.

So the approach is to consider all three options right from the start and build your plan accordingly.

Before we talk about strategy, it's helpful to understand the types of loans you'll encounter.

Not to become an expert—but to understand the landscape in which you'll be making decisions.

The Types of Loans

Here are the most common loan types you will encounter on the award letter or during the financial aid process.

Significant changes were made in 2025, with implementation on July 1, 2026. The information below reflects the most recent changes and may not match what you experienced with an older student.

Federal Student Loans

These are the most common loans offered directly to students.

They typically start around $5,500 in the first year and increase over time.

Some of these loans may be subsidized, meaning the government covers the interest while the student is in school.

Others are unsubsidized, meaning interest begins accruing immediately.

One important detail:

Repayment is tied to enrollment status—not graduation.

If a student drops below half-time enrollment or takes time off, repayment and interest may begin.

Parent PLUS Loans

These are federal loans taken out by parents.

Historically, parents could borrow up to the full remaining cost of attendance after aid.

However, recent changes (effective July 1, 2026) introduced caps on the amount that can be borrowed.

This could leave a larger gap for families to plan around—especially at higher-cost schools.

Interest on Parent PLUS loans begins accruing immediately.

You can choose to defer payments while your student is in school.

But that doesn't mean the interest stops.

It keeps building.

And here's the part that catches families off guard:

When repayment begins, the accumulated interest can be added to the loan balance.

From that point forward, you're paying interest on a balance that is now larger than what you originally borrowed.

In simple terms:

Interest... on interest.

Example:

Let's illustrate this with some straightforward numbers.

Let's say you borrow $20,000 per year for four years.

That's a total of $80,000.

Assuming an interest rate of around 8.5% and deferred payments while your student is in school:

You could easily accumulate $12,000–$18,000 in interest before repayment even begins.

So instead of starting repayment at $80,000...

You may be starting closer to $95,000.

From that point forward, interest is calculated on that higher balance.

Why This Matters:

This is why families often feel their loans "got out of control."

Not because they made a reckless decision—

But because they didn't fully understand how interest works over time.

And remember—this is happening before you've made a single payment.

To be fair, families can choose to pay the interest while the student is in school.

Doing so can significantly reduce the long-term cost.

But most families don't, often because they are already trying to manage everything else.

Private Loans

These are offered by banks and private lenders.

They often allow families to borrow larger amounts, depending on credit and income.

Interest rates vary, and strong credit may result in lower rates than federal loans.

However, private loans typically offer fewer protections than federal loans:

Fewer flexible repayment options
Limited forgiveness provisions
Stricter approval requirements

That doesn't automatically make them bad.

It just means they should be evaluated carefully.

Specifically, private loans often lack the protections found in federal loans, such as income-driven repayment options or guaranteed discharge in certain situations.

Policies vary by lender, so it's important to review the terms carefully.

What Impacts Whether to Use Student Loans

The father mentioned earlier was so desperate because the family had selected a school notorious for not providing any aid.

It turns out the student had other options, but the family chose the school with the recognizable brand name.

School selection played a major role in their situation.

Everything we have discussed so far influences the decision to use student loans.

Why?

Because each of those factors can chip away at the overall cost of college, enabling you to make a strategic decision about loans for the remaining costs.

This gentleman had a good income, but there were definitely opportunities to reduce his AGI.

Had he planned earlier, he likely would have had opportunities to improve the overall picture:

asset positioning
income planning
and school selection.

In that situation, the loan decision may have felt much more manageable and intentional.

I had to tell him there was nothing I could do.

Student loans cannot be an afterthought.

They must be part of the plan.

Strategic Uses of Loans

For me, it comes down to one question:

Does this loan protect your long-term financial future?

If it prevents you from draining retirement accounts, it may be a smart decision.

If it bridges a temporary gap while a larger strategy plays out, it may make sense.

If the career path supports it, it may be justified.

An anesthesiologist may graduate with significant student loans.

But with a high earning potential, the long-term math may still work.

That's not guesswork.

It's something that needs to be carefully modeled.

"How do I know?"

Get someone to model this for you.

Many financial advisors have software—and I am sure there are plenty online—that can help you evaluate your options.

I told the story earlier in the book about the Midwest mom with rental properties.

I was sure our software would recommend selling one of the properties to pay for college.

It turned out that, when we modeled it, it was **$1,000,000 more advantageous for her to take out a loan.**

That is a strategic use of a loan.

If you don't put that level of thought and planning into it, you could end up in a situation like the dad mentioned at the start of the chapter:

Out of options

Credit risk

Desperate

That can leave you saddled with high interest rates, and instead of protecting your future, you're still paying for college in your retirement years.

Who Is Actually Paying This Back?

There is another situation we see all the time that deserves a quick reality check.

Parents take out the loan and assume the student will pay it back later.

On the surface, that sounds reasonable.

"Once they graduate and start working, they can take this over."

That's often the reason families defer payments while the student is in school.

But here's the problem:

The loan is in a parent's name.

Legally, the parent is responsible.

And more importantly…

The payment may not match the student's early career income.

Let's say a student graduates with a degree that leads to a $50,000 starting salary.

Even a modest loan payment can feel significant at that income level.

Now compare that to a student entering a field with a $90,000 or $100,000 starting salary.

Same loan.

Completely different experience.

This is where the conversation shifts from:

"Can we borrow?"

to:

"Does the outcome support the decision?"

There is nothing wrong with choosing a major based on passion.

But we need to be aware of how that decision interacts with cost.

Because when a parent takes on the loan…

and a student is expected to repay it…

You are tying that decision to their future income.

And if those two don't align…

It can create stress for both of you.

This is why return on investment matters.

Not to eliminate options—

But to understand the full picture before making the decision.

A loan doesn't just get repaid.
It gets repaid by someone… with a specific income… at a specific time in their life.

Final Thoughts

Rushing into student loans—or refusing to consider them at all—is risky.

The question is not:

"Should we borrow?"

The better question is:

"Does this borrowing protect or damage our long-term plan?"

Loans are neither inherently good nor inherently bad.

Their impact depends entirely on how thoughtfully they are used.

Because this decision doesn't just affect the next four years.

It affects the next 10, 20, or even 30 years.

36

Study Abroad & International Schools

Every year, I hear some version of this:

"How would it work if my student wants to attend school in another country?"

International programs operate very differently from traditional U.S. colleges, a fact that can quickly lead to trouble for families.

So let's simplify it.

There are really two different conversations here:

- A student attending a U.S. college and studying abroad for a semester or year
- A student attending a foreign university full-time

These are very different scenarios.

Study Abroad Through a U.S. College

This is generally the simpler scenario.

If your student attends a U.S. college and participates in an approved study abroad program, federal aid and institutional aid will often still apply.

That can include:

Federal grants
Federal student loans
Institutional scholarships
Merit aid

But "often" is not the same as "always."

Some schools are generous with study abroad support.

Some are not.

And even when aid transfers, the total cost can still increase significantly.

Families often underestimate:

- Flights
- Housing differences
- Visa costs
- Program fees
- Currency exchange fluctuations
- Travel during breaks
- Higher day-to-day living expenses

One of the biggest risks, however, is a factor families rarely consider:

Credits may not transfer correctly.

A semester abroad that turns into an extra semester—or even a fifth year—can quickly become very expensive.

I am not saying students should avoid studying abroad.

For the right student, it can be an incredible experience.

I am simply saying this:

Carefully evaluate financial and academic logistics before committing.

An Example Where It Made Sense

Recently, I had a student accepted into a well-known, prestigious college.

She has strong career goals and the grades to support them.

At this school, there is a selective program that allows students to study abroad for a year.

But here's why it made sense:

The program is well-established.
Credits transfer smoothly.
Existing grants and loans carry over.
And some international travel and living expenses are covered by an additional grant.

In that situation, my response was simple:

"Do it. Don't think twice."

That is the point.

I am not against studying abroad.

I am against assuming its financial or academic viability without first checking.

Attending a Foreign University Full-Time

This is where things become much more complicated.

Many families assume international universities are automatically less expensive.

Some are.

Some absolutely are not.

And financial aid works very differently outside the United States.

Can You Still Use FAFSA?

Sometimes.

Certain foreign universities participate in the federal student aid system.

That may allow access to:

- Federal student loans
- Pell Grants
- Certain federal programs

But not every international school participates.

And even when they do, the aid options are often much more limited than families expect.

An important point to understand is this:

Most foreign universities do not operate like American private colleges.

Different Funding Models

Many international universities:

Receive government funding
Start with lower tuition
Do not use aggressive merit scholarships
Do not heavily discount tuition to attract students.

That means families often see:

Less institutional aid
Fewer merit opportunities
Smaller overall packages

This is especially true compared with highly competitive U.S. private schools that strategically use financial aid to shape their incoming classes.

But Here's the Twist

Even with less aid, some foreign universities can still be less expensive overall.

For example, a family may compare:

A $95,000-per-year private university in the United States

to

A $30,000-to-$45,000 international program with very little aid.

In that scenario, the international option may still cost substantially less.

That is why this conversation requires actual math—not assumptions.

The "Hidden" Costs to Consider

Families can sometimes underestimate the practical realities of living abroad.

Consider things like:

- International travel
- Housing deposits
- Health insurance requirements
- Visa costs
- Currency fluctuations
- Emergency travel home
- Storage and moving costs
- Limited access to U.S.-style support systems

And while this may sound obvious, it matters:

A student living thousands of miles away may not be able to easily come home for holidays, emergencies, or even support during a tough time.

That emotional and financial reality should be part of the conversation, too.

Final Thoughts

I am not anti-study abroad.

For the right student, international experiences can be life-changing.

But families should understand that international education often follows a very different financial aid model from traditional U.S. colleges.

So don't assume "abroad" automatically means:

Cheaper
More expensive
More generous
Or impossible

It depends on:

The school, country, student, and the family's overall financial picture

As with everything else in this book:

Run the numbers before falling in love with the idea.

And if the numbers work?

It may be one of the best experiences your student will ever have.

37

After the Award: Closing Thoughts

You've done a lot to get here.

You navigated the forms.
You worked through the numbers.
You compared offers.

And you did something many families never realize they can do:

You asked questions.

This entire section has been about what happens after the offer arrives—when the process becomes real.

But by now, I hope you understand something important:

The college price tag is only part of the equation.

A successful outcome is not defined solely by the name of the school or the size of the award.

It's defined by whether your family can navigate the next four years—and the years after that—without sacrificing your long-term financial stability.

Because the reality is:

The money spent on college, once paid, is gone.

Retirement still comes.

Life still happens.

And your financial future still matters.

The ultimate win is not simply an acceptance letter.

It's being able to look back years later and know you helped your student build a future without destroying your own in the process.

That's the real goal.

And that's where we're headed next.

Because getting a better offer matters.

But protecting your family over the next four years—and beyond—

That's the real win.

PART VIII

This Was Never Just About Paying for College

After working with a family—sometimes for years—there comes a point when…

The applications are done.
The forms are submitted.
The offers have come in.
The numbers have been analyzed, compared, and maybe even negotiated.

And just when you think it's all over…

You realize it's not.

There are no more forms to fill out.

No more portals to refresh every five minutes.

But now you're facing the biggest decision of the entire process:

Where do you actually go?

For many families, this is where it gets harder, not easier.

And if you're like most parents, this decision carries a weight that's hard to describe.

Because when you started this process, it probably felt like you were just choosing a school.

But now, you know better.

You're making a financial decision that will impact your family for years—sometimes decades.

You're making decisions about debt, about trade-offs, about what gets prioritized and what gets delayed.

You're making a decision that affects not just this child... but potentially your other children, your retirement, and your long-term security.

That's heavy.

Here's what I want you to understand:

You didn't have to read this book.

But you did.

And because of that, you're not guessing anymore.

Everything we've talked about up to this point—
the strategies, the timing, the school selection, the positioning, the appeals—
was never *just* about getting a better offer.

It was about putting you in a position to make a better decision.

One where you understand not just what something costs...
but what it actually means for your family.

And this is why I've said it before, and I'll say it again:

The award letter is not the finish line.

It's the starting point.

Because once the decision is made…

real life begins.
Bills show up.
Circumstances change.
Students evolve.
Plans shift.

And the strategy you've built?

It doesn't stop.

It continues.

So in this final section, we're going to talk about what happens next.

What it actually looks like to live with this decision over the next four years.

How to protect your family while you're paying for college.

And how to define what a real "win" looks like—beyond acceptance letters and financial aid packages.

Because in the end…

This was never *just* about paying for college.

It was about doing it in a way that doesn't cost you everything else.

38

The 4-Year Reality

I've touched on this throughout the book, but this is where it becomes real:

The award letter—and the strategy behind it—are for year one.

You still have four years ahead of you.

In most cases:

You'll complete the FAFSA every year.
Many schools will require the CSS Profile annually.

So why did we spend so much time preparing for the first year?

Because the first year sets the tone.

But after that…

Life happens.

Sometimes it's positive.

Sometimes it's messy.

In this chapter, we'll discuss how to live with this decision—and how to keep making the best of it over time.

The Award Letter

The award letter represents year one.

Some elements may carry forward for all four years—but not all of them.

Schools understand that life changes.

That's why most offers are not guaranteed unconditionally.

Each year, when you submit updated financial forms, the school evaluates whether your situation has changed.

If your income increases significantly…
If your assets change meaningfully…

Your aid can change.

Small changes typically don't move the needle much.

But large changes can.

In some cases—especially at well-funded private schools—a sudden increase in assets can shift the conversation entirely.

We've seen situations where a family receives an inheritance or experiences a significant liquidity event. While the aid formula may not immediately change, the school becomes acutely aware of this increased capacity.

That's when conversations around giving, contributions, or "supporting the institution" can emerge—sometimes subtly, sometimes overtly.

It doesn't happen everywhere.

But it occurs enough that you should be aware of it.

The takeaway is this:

Your financial aid strategy isn't just for the first year.

It continues every year.

Renewal Requirements

Some parts of your award come with conditions.

For example:

- Academic scholarships often require a minimum GPA.
- Aid may require full-time enrollment.
- Some funding is tied to a specific major or department.

If a

- Student drops too many classes,
- falls below GPA requirements,
- or changes academic direction,

that aid may be reduced—or lost.

"Directional Accuracy" matters here.

If a student shifts from engineering to business, certain funding may not follow.

A change within a department? Usually fine.

A change across departments? Sometimes not.

Do you need to worry about this constantly?

No.

But you do need to be aware of it.

Because this is the kind of detail that tends to arise in real-world conversations.

Your student might say:

"I'm thinking about dropping this class."
"I might switch majors."
"This is harder than I expected."

Totally normal.

But now you have context.

You can have a more informed conversation—not just about academics, but about the financial impact of those decisions.

Because what feels like a small change in the moment... can have a ripple effect on aid.

Life Happens

I mentioned earlier that roughly one-third of students will experience a financial disruption during college.

That's a significant number.

Hopefully, it doesn't happen to your family.

But if it does, you're not stuck.

The same concepts we discussed in the appeals section still apply.

You notify the school of a change in circumstances.
You provide documentation.
You ask for a review.

And this may happen more than once.

That's normal.

It might feel repetitive.

It might feel frustrating.

But it's part of the process.

You're not starting over.

You're continuing the conversation.

One way to think about it:

Your award letter is a scene.

The next four years... that's the movie.

And now, you're not just watching it.

You're helping shape how it plays out.

39

Protecting the Family

After everything we've discussed, this is where it becomes very real.

Because at some point, every family ends up asking the same question:

"How do we make this work… without hurting everything else?"

And that's the part that doesn't get talked about enough.

There are five areas of financial loss.

This is where families tend to lose money unknowingly and unnecessarily.

These are:
Taxes
Mortgage
Qualified plans
Major expenses (cars, weddings, vacations, etc.)
College

College stands out on this list.

Why?

The others are somewhat obvious:

You can pay too much in taxes.
Have a bad mortgage interest rate.
Invest poorly in your retirement plans.
You can spend too much or make bad decisions on major purchases.

College is unique because it touches all of them.

There is a direct correlation between your AGI and how much you will pay for college and in taxes.

Many people consider taking out a second mortgage on their house to pay for college.

Some — and I do not recommend this — borrow or withdraw money from their retirement accounts.

Often, budgets for major purchases are redirected to college expenses.

And then there are the long-term financial implications of overpaying for college.

The "We'll figure it out" approach often costs families not just thousands in the first year, but potentially tens of thousands in the years to come.

The Costly Tradeoffs

I hear families talk about the trade-offs they will make to afford college.

They don't usually call them trade-offs.

It sounds more like:

"We won't take vacations."
"I'll work a few more years."

"We'll borrow against the house."
"We'll pull from the 401(k)."

But each of those is a trade.

You are trading long-term security… for a short-term decision.

Yes—even vacations.

Not just financially, but mentally. Emotionally. Relationally.

At first, it doesn't feel like a big deal.

You pay the first semester.

Then the next.

Maybe you open a line of credit.

Then something breaks at home.

Then the next bill comes.

Then the Parent PLUS loan.

And before you realize it…
you're managing a situation that has slowly accumulated.

Not because you made a bad decision—
but because you made a series of reasonable ones.

That's how financial creep happens.

And that's what this book is trying to help you avoid.

The Retirement Tradeoff

There is an entire section of this book dedicated to this topic, so I won't rehash it.

But I do want to remind you of something simple:

They offer loans for school.

They do not offer loans for retirement.

That's why I tell families:

Fund your future first.
Finance their education if you must.

Because all of the options we talked about earlier—

Home equity
401(k) loans
IRA withdrawals
School loans
Draining savings

—those don't just solve today's problem.

They create tomorrow's.

And the reality is:

You are much closer to retirement than to the beginning of your career.

This is no longer a distant concern.

It's a near-term one.

Siblings

It's common for me to meet with families who already have one child in college.

They've taken loans.
Used the 529.
Maybe tapped home equity.

And now the next child is coming up, and they're worried.

This happens because of what I call financial creep.

Some of it comes from life.
Some misunderstand the original offer.

Either way, the plan they started with…
and the reality they're living in now…
are often very different.

And here's the key:

Every decision you make for the first child sets the precedent for the next.

That's where this becomes even more important.

"What Can We Afford?"

In most areas of life, affordability comes down to one question:

Can we make the payment?

With a home, there's usually long-term value.

With a car, the impact is limited if you stay within reason.

But college is different.

There's no appreciating asset.

There is no guaranteed return.

And the timing—so close to retirement—magnifies every decision.

So the question isn't:

"Can we afford the payment?"

It's:

"Can we do this without damaging our future?"

> **"Can we do this without damaging our future?"**

That's a very different question.

Here are three better ones to ask:

Which school creates the least long-term stress?
Which school has the smallest impact on our retirement timeline?
Will we still feel good about this decision in 5–10 years?

Because the goal is not just to get them through college.

It's to do it without compromising everything else.

At some point, you're going to want to slow down.

That part is predictable.

What's not predictable is how this college decision will affect your ability to do it.

"No" Is An Answer

I don't know many parents who appreciate unsolicited parenting advice.

This is not that.

However, I do want you to know that after helping families for many years, **I've never seen a single case where a student ended up in a horrible situation because they went to their third-choice school instead of their first.**

If the college list was built correctly, all of the top choices were a good environmental fit for the student and offered their major.

Why do I bring this up?

Because saying no, in order to protect your financial future—which is also their financial future—is an acceptable answer.

We love to say yes to our kids.

I know I do.

At the outset of this book, I mentioned that families talk about how hard their student worked to get into their dream school and therefore feel compelled to make it happen.

But that isn't always financially viable.

I had a family a few years ago navigating a complex remarriage situation.

The student's top choice was SMU.

Second choice: Loyola Marymount.

LMU offered a generous package.

SMU offered nothing.

The student insisted on SMU.

The parents said yes.

The financial impact was massive.

And at their age—early 50s—there wasn't much time to recover.

Would the student have received a great education at either school?

Absolutely.

That's the point.

Saying no isn't failure.

Sometimes it's the most responsible decision you can make.

The goal is to find the school that provides them with:

A reasonable chance of acceptance.
A major they want to pursue and an environmental fit.
Affordability.

If you achieve those three, you protect your family's future.

It's Not All On You

This chapter has focused on your role as the parent—

protecting the family, making the decision, managing the long-term impact.

But this responsibility doesn't rest entirely on your shoulders.

Some of it belongs to the person receiving the degree.

In the next chapter, we'll talk about the student's role—

how they can influence the outcome, and what they need to understand to make better decisions.

Because they don't know what they don't know.

This is where we help them understand.

40

Helping Your Student Protect Their Future

Up to this point, we've been discussing your role as the parent.

But this decision doesn't belong to you alone.

Whether they realize it or not...
your student is also living with the outcome of this decision.

This chapter isn't about expecting your student to pay for college.

That's a personal decision each family makes.

This chapter is about something else.

It's about the conversations most students never hear.

School counselors talk about prestige, degrees, careers, and earning potential.

Those are important—I talk about them too.

But very few people discuss the long-term financial impact of the cost of college.

Questions like:

How long will it take to pay off student loans?
Will early career income realistically support those payments?
How does this decision affect the family's long-term financial picture?

And yes…

even inheritance.

I know—that one can sting a little.

But it matters.

Not because your student is thinking about it now—

but because it will affect them later.

This Is Their Life Too

The college decision is a bit of a perfect storm.

They're thinking about:

Leaving home.
Moving to a new place.
Being away from friends.
Figuring out what they want to do with their life.

And on top of that…

they're likely turning 18.

Which is when you start to hear:

"I'm an adult now."

And you're thinking, "Oh… just wait."

Add in friendships, relationships, pressure from peers, and messages like:

"If you don't go to a great school, you won't make good money…"

It's a lot.

No wonder they have strong opinions.

And sometimes, the opposite happens.

You ask where they want to go…

and all you get is a shrug and:

"I don't know."

Either way, this is a major turning point in their life.

So let's talk about a few things they're probably not hearing but should.

The Inheritance Factor

Yes, I'm going there.

I don't like thinking about my own mortality any more than you do.

But it's part of the reality.

We've talked about the three ways to pay for college:

Income
Assets
Debt

Each of these impacts their future.

Maybe not today… but eventually.

And sometimes, that "eventually" arrives at a meaningful time—like when their own children are getting ready for college.

Teenagers don't naturally think long-term.

That's normal.

But that doesn't mean the conversation isn't worth having.

Student Levers

Students often desire independence.

That's part of this stage of life—and part of what makes college exciting.

What many don't realize is how much control they actually have over the cost of their experience.

Here are a few areas where they can make a meaningful impact:

Graduation Time
The faster they graduate, the less it costs.

It's a simple equation—but it requires focus and planning.

And it can influence school choice since graduation rates are public.

Part-Time Work
Having some income helps—both practically and personally.

I often recommend restaurant work:

flexible hours, good pay, and valuable life skills.

It also raises an important question:

If they choose a small school in a small town…

will those opportunities even exist?

Resident Assistant (RA)
This can significantly reduce housing costs.

Some of my students say they get paid to do homework at night.

Teaching Assistant (TA)

Working with professors can open doors—academically and professionally.

These aren't just side benefits.

They're part of the decision.

And they're completely within the student's control.

Graduate School Reality

Graduate school is outside the scope of this book.

But it's worth mentioning.

At that level, students are treated as independent.

The loans are theirs.

That changes everything.

This is why some students choose a more affordable undergraduate path and save the "big name" for graduate school.

The decisions they make now can create flexibility later… or limit it.

Staying Focused

Students control their focus.

Will there be distractions?

Of course.

As one parent told me about a very prestigious, faith-based school:

"If they want to find it... they'll find it."

And that's true.

Should they enjoy college?

Absolutely.

We want them to grow.
We want them to have fun.
(Even if we don't want all the details.)

But they also need to stay on track.

Because the decisions that feel small—

dropping a class,
changing majors late,
letting grades slip—

can become very expensive over time.

Partnership, Not Pressure

This doesn't need to feel like a burden for your student.

But they also shouldn't be completely unaware of it.

They're going to have a voice in this decision—

likely a strong one.

The goal isn't to shut that down.

It's to elevate the conversation.

Instead of 'We can't afford this,' try:

"Here's what this choice means over time."
"Here's what we're balancing as a family."
"Here's where you can help influence the outcome."

Because, as you've likely taught them:

The best decisions come from understanding—not pressure.

And that understanding is what changes everything.

Because at the end of the day…
this decision isn't just about where they go.

It's about how they—and your family—live with that decision afterward.

41

The Ultimate Win

We've covered a lot together in this book.

And if you're still here…

It's because this decision matters to you.

We started with that moment—

Your student is excited about where they want to go…

and you're quietly wondering how you'll pay for it.

By now, you've realized something important:

The goal isn't to manage the worry.

It's to remove it.

This book has shown you that, with the right planning, even financially successful families don't have to feel financially broken by college.

While paying less is important... you've also seen that this was never just about saving money for a few years.

It's about protecting everything that comes after.

At the beginning, it may have felt like the goal was simple:

Get into a great school...
and figure out how to pay for it.

But hope isn't a strategy.

So we shifted the goal.

Plan ahead.

Protect your future.

And still position your student for success.

The real win is when they get a great education... and you don't have to sacrifice your future to make it happen.

The Noisy Misinformation

A big part of this process is learning how to tune out the noise.

You've probably heard it:

"You won't qualify for anything."
"My kid got into a top school—we'll figure it out."
"State schools are the only affordable option."
"Don't even bother filling out the FAFSA."

The truth is:

No two situations are the same.

And when someone is celebrating where their student is going…

You're not seeing the full picture.

You're not seeing the debt.
The trade-offs.
The stress behind the scenes.

What looks like a win from the outside…

doesn't always feel like one in reality.

You now have the tools to avoid that.

4 Parts to the Ultimate Win

So what is the ultimate win?

If you can look back on this decision in a few years…

and feel good about both your student's path and your family's situation,

that's it.

That outcome comes down to four things we've talked about throughout this book.

Your Student Thrives
They stay focused but still enjoy the experience.
They finish on time.

The Degree Makes Sense
We don't expect them to have everything figured out at 14.
We're looking for a clear sense of direction.
A degree they enjoy.
One that they can actually use.
One that opens doors.

The Cost is Sustainable
You're not making unreasonable sacrifices.
You're not panicking when the bill comes.
You're not hoping it all works out.
You know it will.

Your Financial Future Is Still Intact
Retirement is still on track.
You're not working years longer than you planned.

You've protected the future you worked so hard to build.

When all four of these factors align...
that's when you know you got it right.

That is the ultimate win.

What Does That Look Like For You?

In my workshops, I often ask families to picture this:

Your student is at a school where they're thriving.

You're paying far less than you expected.

And you're not stressed.

Then I ask:

What are you doing instead?

Building your business?
Taking more time off?
Traveling?
Investing?

The answer is different for everyone.

But here's what it shouldn't be:

Working longer hours.
Carrying more stress.
Putting pressure on your home life.
Worrying about how you'll manage it all for another child.

The Kitchen Table – Revisited

We started with that moment:

Your teenager bursts into the kitchen and says,

"Mom. Dad. I figured it out. I want to go to USC."

Before, your thought might have been:

"Oh crap… how are we going to pay for this?"

Now?

You've done the work.

You've planned your income and assets.
You've built the right school list.
You've evaluated and appealed the offers.

So instead, you say:

"That's wonderful, honey. We're so happy for you. Let's celebrate."

Same kitchen.

Completely different conversation.

If You Want Some Help

If you're reading this and thinking:

"This makes sense… but I don't want to do it alone…"

That's exactly why we built Auxilium College Advisors.

Whether you need:

guidance,
tools,
or hands-on support,

you don't have to figure this out by yourself.

https://www.gettuitionpaid.com/90k

Because at the end of the day…

This was never just about paying for college.

It's about doing it in a way that protects everything else.

You've got this.

College Funding Glossary & Guide

This glossary is designed as a quick reference rather than a complete dictionary.

Some entries include related topics and chapter references to help you revisit important concepts throughout the book.

You may notice that some terms include **"Primary Discussion"** sections, while others include **"Related Topics."**

Primary Discussion points you to the main discussion where the concept is introduced.

Related Topics connect you to other chapters where that concept appears in a different context or becomes part of a larger strategy.

Not every term includes additional references. Some concepts are straightforward and only need a definition, while others appear throughout the book and benefit from deeper exploration.

AGI (Adjusted Gross Income)
The income figure most commonly used in federal financial aid calculations. For the tax year discussed in this book, it is found on Line 11a of IRS Form 1040.
Primary Discussion:
Chapter 5 - Income - When Income is Considered (p. 27)
Related Topics:
Income Timing (p. 7)
AGI & W2 Employees (p. 130)
AGI & Business Owners (p. 133)

Common Application
A standardized application form that is accepted by many colleges.

Cost of Attendance (COA)
The total estimated cost of attending a college for a year, including tuition, fees, room and board, books, and living expenses.
Primary Discussion:
Chapter 1 - Cost Dilemma (p. 4)
Related Topics:
The Award Letter - COA Breakdown (p. 280)

Cost Segregation
A tax strategy often used by rental property owners that accelerates depreciation by identifying parts of a property that can be depreciated faster than the building itself. This may reduce taxable income during key financial aid years.
Primary Discussion:
Chapter 23 - Advanced Income Strategies - Rental Properties (p. 194)

CSS Profile
A financial aid application used by some colleges and universities to award non-federal aid, administered by the College Board.
Primary Discussion:
Chapter 3 - Two Applications. Two Systems. (p. 15)
Related Topics:
CSS & Retirement Accounts (p. 36)
CSS & Primary Residence (p. 38)

Is the CSS Optional? (p. 89)
Divorce, Separation & Financial Aid Reality (p. 244)

CSS Non-Custodial Parent Waiver (NCP Waiver)
A request made to a CSS Profile school to exclude the non-custodial parent's financial information due to circumstances such as abandonment, abuse, or inability to contact the parent.
Primary Discussion:
Chapter 29 - Divorce, Separation, & Financial Aid Reality (p. 245)

Early Action (EA)
A non-binding college application process in which students apply early and receive decisions before the regular admission dates.

Early Decision (ED)
A binding college application process in which students apply to their first-choice school early and agree to attend if admitted.

Expected Family Contribution (EFC)
Historical term replaced by the Student Aid Index (SAI). See ***SAI****.*

Federal Pell Grant
Need-based federal grant program for undergraduate students with exceptional financial need.
Primary Discussion:
Chapter 11 - Pell Grant Definition (p. 74)

Federal Student Aid (FSA)
The federal government's office overseeing student financial aid programs.

Financial Aid Package
The combination of grants, scholarships, loans, and work-study awarded to a student to help pay for college.

Free Application for Federal Student Aid (FAFSA)
The standard form for applying for federal and state need-based financial aid.
Primary Discussion:

Chapter 3 - Two Applications. Two Systems. (p. 15)
Related Topics:
FAFSA & Retirement Accounts (p. 36)
FAFSA & Primary Residence (p. 37)
"There is No Point in Filling Out the FAFSA" (p. 81)
Divorce, Separation, & Financial Aid Reality (p.240)
Appeals & Negotiation (p. 296)
Studying Abroad (p. 320)

Gift Aid
Financial aid that does not need to be repaid, typically including grants and scholarships. I often refer to it as "free money."

Grant
Financial aid that does not need to be repaid, often based on financial need.

Institutional Aid
Financial aid provided directly by a college or university rather than through federal or state programs. This may include grants, scholarships, tuition discounts, and school-specific assistance.
Primary Discussion:
Chapter 11 - "We Make Too Much" (p. 76)
Related Topics:
School Methodologies (p. 202)
School Selection (p. 212)

Institutional Methodology (IM)
The financial aid methodology often used by CSS Profile schools to evaluate a family's ability to pay beyond federal FAFSA formulas. (p.202)

K-1 Income
Income reported on IRS Schedule K-1 from partnerships, S corporations, or certain trusts. The income may or may not have been distributed to the owner.

Loan
Money borrowed from the government or a private lender to pay for college, which must be repaid with interest.

Primary Discussion:
Chapter 35 - Student Loans (p. 307)

MAGI (Modified Adjusted Gross Income)
A variation of Adjusted Gross Income used in certain tax and financial calculations. Some schools may review MAGI in addition to AGI when evaluating overall financial strength.

Merit-Based Aid
Financial aid awarded based on a student's academic achievements, talents, or skills.
Primary Discussion:
Chapter 8 - School Selection (p. 53)

Need-Based Aid
Financial aid awarded based on a student's financial need, as determined by the FAFSA and/or CSS Profile.
Primary Discussion:
Chapter 8 - School Selection (p. 53)

Need-Aware Admission
An admissions policy where a student's financial need may be considered as part of the admissions process, especially when schools are managing enrollment and financial aid budgets.
Primary Discussion:
Chapter 25 - School Selection (p. 211)

Need-Blind Admission
An admissions policy where a student's financial need is not considered during the admissions decision process.
Primary Discussion:
Chapter 25 - School Selection (p. 211)

Net Price Calculator
A tool on a college's website that allows students and families to estimate their net price (cost of attendance minus financial aid).
Primary Discussion:

Chapter 27 - NPC Definition (p. 232)

Net Price
The estimated cost of attending a college after subtracting grants and scholarships. Unlike "total aid," net price does not include loans as a discount.

Parent PLUS Loan
A federal loan available to parents of undergraduate students to help cover education costs not already covered by financial aid. Interest begins accruing immediately, and the repayment responsibility belongs to the parent.
Primary Discussion:
Chapter 35 - Types of Loans (p. 310)

Phantom Income
Taxable income reported on a tax return, even though no actual cash was received by the taxpayer. Common with certain business structures, partnerships, or K-1 income.
Primary Discussion:
Chapter 31 - Businesses & Phantom Income (p. 267)

Professional Judgment (PJ)
A formal process that allows a financial aid office to review special financial circumstances not fully reflected on the FAFSA or CSS Profile. Examples may include job loss, medical expenses, business downturns, or other major life changes.
Primary Discussion:
Chapter 31 - When the Numbers Don't Reflect Reality (p. 261)

Professional Review
Another term commonly used for Professional Judgment. This process allows a financial aid office to reevaluate a family's financial situation due to special circumstances or updated information.
Primary Discussion:
Chapter 31 - When the Numbers Don't Reflect Reality (p. 261)

Rolling Admissions
Colleges that review applications and make admissions decisions on an ongoing basis.

SAI (Student Aid Index)
The number calculated from the FAFSA that schools use to help determine eligibility for federal financial aid. Formerly known as the Expected Family Contribution (EFC).
Primary Discussion:
Chapter 3 - The Number That Drives Everything (p. 17)
Related Topics:
The Pell Grant & SAI (p. 74)
The Impact of Assets on SAI (p. 148)

Scholarship
Financial aid awarded based on academic merit, talents, financial need, or criteria established by the scholarship provider.
Primary Discussion:
Chapter 14 - Scholarships (p. 98)

Stafford Loans
Common name for federal Direct Loans available to undergraduate and graduate students. These may be subsidized or unsubsidized depending on eligibility.
Primary Discussion:
Chapter 35 - Types of Loans (p. 310)

Student Aid Report (SAR):
Historically, student received a summary of FAFSA information after submission. Under the newer FAFSA processes, students more commonly receive FAFSA Submission Summaries, though many families and professionals still use the term "SAR."

Subsidized Loan
A federal student loan for which the government pays the interest while the student is in school and during grace and deferment periods.

Tuition Discounting (Merit Discounting)

A strategy used by colleges in which scholarships or merit aid effectively reduce the published tuition price to attract desirable students.

Primary Discussion:

Chapter 25 - Merit Aid (p. 211)

Unsubsidized Loan

A federal student loan for which the student is responsible for paying all the interest, which accrues from the time the loan is disbursed.

Waitlist

A list of applicants who may be admitted if space becomes available after the initial round of acceptances.

Work-Study

A federal program that provides part-time jobs for undergraduate and graduate students with financial need, allowing them to earn money to help pay for educational expenses.

Primary Discussion:

Chapter 32 - Understanding the Award Letter (p. 279)

Yield Rate

The percentage of admitted students who ultimately choose to enroll at a college. Schools closely monitor yield because it helps them predict enrollment, manage housing and class sizes, and make financial aid decisions. A student who appears more likely to enroll may sometimes receive a more competitive offer.

About the Author

Ivana Cummins helps families navigate the often-confusing world of college funding, financial aid, and college planning.

A graduate of the University of California, Santa Barbara, Ivana originally planned to become a teacher before pursuing a successful legal career. Today, she works with families across the country through Auxilium College Advisors, helping them understand financial aid systems, identify opportunities, and make informed decisions about paying for college.

As the daughter of Italian immigrants, Ivana was raised with a deep appreciation for education, hard work, and opportunity. She is passionate about helping families avoid costly mistakes and gain clarity during one of the most important financial decisions they will ever make.

Ivana lives in Southern California with her husband, Dominic, and their family.

Learn more at GetTuitionPaid.com.

instagram.com/get_tuition_paid

facebook.com/gettuitionpaid

Additional Resources

Thank you for reading *The $90,000 Question.*

If you'd like additional tools and resources to help you navigate the college funding process, we've created a free companion resource:

The College Planning Timeline

A practical roadmap covering:

- Financial aid planning
- College selection
- Academic preparation
- Scholarship planning
- Key milestones from middle school through senior year

Download your free copy at:

GetTuitionPaid.com/90k

www.ingramcontent.com/pod-product-compliance
Lightning Source LLC
LaVergne TN
LVHW052030200926
848481LV00005B/1633